# HISTORICAL BACKGROUND

During the Viking incursions of the 9th and 10th centuries, England and north-western France suffered particularly. In or about 911, Charles III (the Simple), King of the West Franks, was forced to allow a chieftain called Rollo, operating in the Seine valley, to settle his men on territory in what is now upper or eastern Normandy bounded by the rivers Bresle, Epte, Avre and Dives. The Treaty of St.-Clair-sur-Epte has come down in a semi-legendary form. In return for the gift of land the king would be a nominal overlord, possibly recognising Rollo's conversion to Christianity and receiving military aid. The new state would also act as a buffer against further raiding. Rollo soon expanded his territories into lower or western Normandy. In 924 the Bessin and districts of Sées and Exmes were granted to him, whilst his son and successor, William Longsword, gained the Cotentin and Avranchin in 933.

The newly defined boundaries fitted less those of the Carolingian province of Neustria than the old Roman province of the Second Lyonnaise. From this, Rouen had become the metropolitan head of the province and remained as the most important city of the new Norman duchy. The new settlers spoke Scandinavian and had come to a country in which the native population was Gallo-Roman with an overculture of Germanic Frankish lords. Rollo at least seems to have been Norwegian but the settlement of Vikings soon saw the new creation given the name of Normandy—land of the Northmen. It was not long before the Normans in upper Normandy, their ducal base at Rouen, began to adapt themselves to French custom and largely adopted what is now termed the Old French tongue. In lower Normandy Scandinavian customs tended to linger and for a time the two areas lived uneasily with one another. This state was ended after a revolt of lords, largely in Lower Normandy, was crushed at Val-és-Dunes in 1047 by the youthful Duke William II and King Henry I of France. Thereafter William set about establishing a ducal presence in the west at Caen and tied his lords more closely, assisted by the old unifying boundaries of metropolitan Rouen.

*Knights of the early 11th century lunge at one another with lances, as portrayed in 'The Vision of Habukuk' from the northern French Bible of St Vaast. The horses are shown at a standstill as opposed to the galloping stance usual in the later 11th and 12th century. It also highlights the use of the lance as a thrusting weapon rather than couched under the arm in the charge. Note the mail neck-guard on the left-hand figure who otherwise appears to be unarmoured, suggesting that, unusual at this date, the mail is possibly attached to the brim of the helmet. (Bibliothèque Municipale, Arras, Ms 435)*

The Norman dukes had always had an uneasy relationship with the French king. As nominal overlord they owed him feudal fealty and whilst Normandy was in formation the king was content. After Duke William's victory at Val-és-Dunes the new stability disturbed the monarch who decided the duchy was becoming too powerful for comfort. He therefore allied himself with the Angevins on the southern borders of Normandy. Anjou would always be a rival for the land along the southern marches and here lay perhaps the most contested border. In 1054 and again in 1057 King Henry, allied with Count Geoffrey of Anjou, led forces into Normandy. He was beaten off both at Mortemer and Varaville, leaving William in a strong position.

When William's second cousin, Edward of England, died in 1066 the Duke swore he had been named as heir during that king's previous exile in Normandy. The Angevin count and the French king had both died in 1060; the new king was a minor in the wardship of William's father-in-law; the Bretons to the west had been given a show of strength. Under these auspicious circumstances the duke made his bid for the English crown. Harold, the new king, was beaten near Hastings and William at a stroke had brought a new and rich kingdom under the sway of Normandy. As king of England he now increased his power enormously. Unfortunately the cohesion of this situation was never strong. His sons squabbled as each wished to control all. William Rufus succeeded his father in 1087 but died whilst hunting in the New Forest in 1100. His young brother, Henry, took the throne and imprisoned his elder brother, Robert of Normandy. Tragedy robbed Henry of a male heir when his own son drowned in the White Ship disaster in the Channel. Consequently civil war broke out on Henry's death in 1135 between his daughter, Mathilda, and his nephew, Stephen, who had been made king by barons hostile to a woman's rule.

The war made the lords aware of how difficult it was to owe fealty to a duke of Normandy and an English king. On Stephen's death in 1154 Mathilda's son, Henry, took the crown. Henry, who had inherited the county of Anjou from his father, marked the beginning of the Plantagenet line of kings; England was now part of an Angevin empire that stretched from the borders of Scotland to the Pyrenees. The country, of course, was still essentially an Anglo-Norman realm. However, now lords were forced to renounce dual control of cross-Channel possessions, either settling in England or Normandy. It was the French king, Philip II Augustus, who finally wrested the duchy from the control of the English crown. Unsuccessful against Henry's bellicose son, Richard the Lionheart, he nevertheless managed to take it from Richard's brother, John.

The energy of the Normans carried them beyond Normandy and England. At the same time as adventurers were conquering England, other Normans were carving out kingdoms in southern Italy and Sicily. Mercenaries had fought in a revolt against the Byzantines in Italy as early as 1017 and began settling in about 1029 but it was not until 1041 that Robert Guiscard and his followers began to seize land for themselves. The Pope recognised their possessions around Apulia and Calabria in 1059, hoping to use the Normans as a counter to pressures from the emperor in the German lands to the north. By 1071

*Circular shields were used until about AD 1000 when they were supplemented by the kite-shaped variety. This survivor is from the Gokstad ship burial in Norway and dates to about 900. Although a funeral piece it was probably made in similar fashion to war shields. It is constructed from butted planks, presumably glued together, and is fitted with a typical Scandinavian low hemispherical boss. The metal bands at rear are modern supports. (University Museum of National Antiquities, Oslo. Photograph: L.Pedersen)*

*The cutting sword usually had a fuller running for much of the blade's length. These examples are fitted with a tea-cosy pommel from as early as the 10th century, a brazil-nut pommel, popular from the late 10th century until about 1150, while the 12th century sword on the right has a disc pommel and is possibly Italian. (By kind permission of James Pickthorn. Reproduced by permission of the Trustees of the Wallace Collection, London)*

they had taken Bari, effectively ending Byzantine control. The invasion of Sicily began in 1060 and was not completed for 31 years. Initially ruled separately, the states came under one authority in 1127, being recognised as a kingdom three years later. In about 1134 a successful invasion of Tunisia was under way, taking advantage of internal feuding between the Zirid rulers. From 1148 until its collapse by 1160 the Normans ruled an area from Tunis to the Gulf of Sirte. Despite attempts to attack the Greek mainland and the capture of Thessaloniki, the Siculo-Norman kingdom was riven by discord which ended in 1194 with the invasion by the German Hohenstaufen Emperor, Henry VI.

Normans were also very much in evidence in the 1st Crusade. Two of the leaders were Duke Robert of Normandy and Bohemond of Taranto with his contingent of south Italian fighters. Bohemond went on to set up the principality of Antioch in Syria. Situated on a trade route and the richest Crusader state, the port of Lattakieh was the final town of the principality to fall to the Muslims in 1287.

# CHRONOLOGY

**911** Treaty of St.-Clair-sur-Epte. Rollo becomes first duke of Normandy.

**931** Death of Rollo. Succeeded by his son, William I Longsword.

**942** Death of William I. Succeeded by his son, Richard the Fearless.

**996** Death of Richard. Succeeded by his son, Richard II, the Good.

**1017** (?) First Norman mercenaries arrive in southern Italy.

**1026** Death of Richard II. Succeeded by his son, Richard III.

**1027** Death of Richard III. Succeeded by his brother, Robert the Magnificent.

**1028** (?) Birth of William the Conqueror.

**1035** Death of Robert. Succeeded by his illegitimate son as Duke William II.

**1041** Battle of Monte Maggiore. Italo-Norman mercenary rebels defeat Byzantine army.

**1047** Battle of Val-és-Dunes. Duke William defeats Norman rebels.

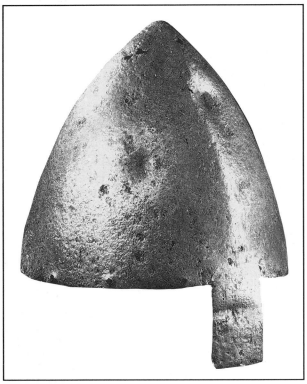

*This typical 'Norman' helmet is actually from Olmütz in Moravia though probably contemporary in date. Of one-piece construction it has a slight medial ridge and an integral nasal. The rivet holes round the lower edge would have secured an internal lining. (Hofjagd- und Rüstkammer, Vienna)*

*This segmented helmet is variously reported as found in northern France and in the River Thames. The nasal is a restoration. Many such helmets shown in the Bayeux Tapestry suggest that the nasal was usually attached to a brow-band, the segment joints being at front, sides and back. (Metropolitan Museum of Art, New York)*

**1053** Battle of Civitate. Apulian Normans defeat Papal army.

**1054** Battle of Mortemer. Normans defeat invading forces of Henry I of France and Geoffrey of Anjou.

**1057** Battle of Varaville. Normans destroy rearguard of invading forces of King Henry and Geoffrey of Anjou.

**1060** Norman conquest of Sicily begins.

**1066** 28 Sept. Duke William invades England.

**1066** 14 Oct. Battle of Hastings. King Harold of England defeated by Duke William.

**1066** 25 Dec. William is crowned King of England in Westminster Abbey.

**1070** Final major revolts in England put down.

**1071** Capture of Bari in southern Italy by the Normans.

**1072** Capture of Palermo in Sicily by the Normans.

**1079** William defeated at Gerberoi by his son, Robert.

**1081** Battle of Durazzo. Italo-Norman army of Robert Guiscard and son, Bohemond of Taranto, defeats Byzantine army.

**1087** 9 Sept. Death of King William I. William Rufus succeeds as William II. Robert becomes Duke of Normandy.

**1091** Norman conquest of Sicily completed.

**1097** Battle of Dorylaeum. Forces of 1st Crusade, including Italo-Normans of Bohemond, hard pressed until 2nd column surprises and defeats Turks.

**1098** Bohemond captures Antioch

**1100** Bohemond becomes Prince of Antioch.
William II killed in New Forest. Younger brother Henry becomes King of England.

**1106** Battle of Tinchebrai. Henry I defeats and

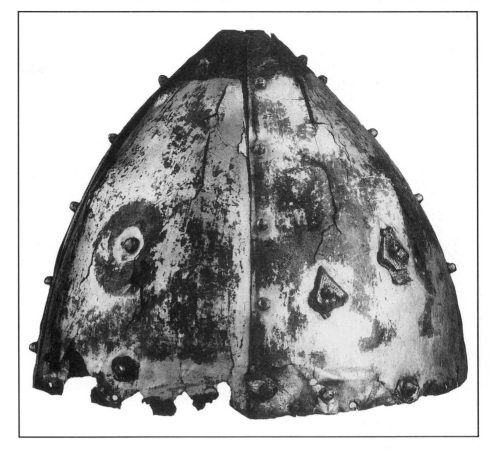

► *A Polish helmet composed of four segments riveted together, a type common in the west. This example is gilded. (Liverpool Museum, on loan to the Royal Armouries)*

▼ *The helmet of St Wenceslas in Prague is traditionally associated with that saint and may be of 10th-century date. Although the skull has been raised in one piece the nasal is attached to an applied brow-band. The latter bears decoration which has led some to believe the helmet was originally from northern Europe.*

imprisons his brother, Duke Robert of Normandy.

1118  Battle of Alençon. Henry I defeated by Geoffrey of Anjou whilst trying to relieve the castle.

1119  Battle of Brémule. Henry I defeats invading force of Louis VI of France.

1124  Battle of Bourgthéroulde. Household knights of Henry I defeat rebel Waleran of Meulan.

1132  Battle of Nocera. Roger II of Sicily defeated by Apulian Norman rebels.

1135  Death of Henry I. Civil war breaks out in England over disputed succession between Henry's nephew, Stephen, and his daughter, Mathilda.

1138  Battle of the Standard (Northallerton). Army of Stephen defeats David I of Scotland.

1141  Battle of Lincoln. Robert of Gloucester and rebel forces come to relief of city, defeat and capture Stephen. Exchange of Stephen for Robert when the latter captured trying to break out of Winchester later that year.

# APPEARANCE AND EQUIPMENT

Many, if not most, items of the dress and armour worn and the weapons used by the Norman knight could be seen in much of north-western Europe at this time and were not specific to him alone. When good sword blades might be imported and fresh armour could be had from the battlefield, such intermixing of pieces is hardly surprising.

### The 10th and 11th centuries

Next to his skin the Norman knight wore a linen shirt which was pulled on over the head. Underwear consisted of a baggy pair of long breeches or braies which often reached the ankles and were tied under the shirt with a waist girdle. They tended to be close fitting from knee to ankle. Woollen or linen knee-length stockings or chausses might be worn over them, often having an embroidered band at the top which may have served as a garter. Very occasionally the chausses reached above the knee; a few were fitted with a stirrup instead of a foot. Leg bandages were sometimes worn over the braies or chausses, bound spirally from the foot to below the knee. The criss-cross method of fastening was a style reserved for the nobility. Shoes were of leather and closed with thongs which passed through slits cut in the shoe.

Over the shirt came the tunic, again put on over the head. It was knee or calf-length with long sleeves that sometimes were puckered at the wrist, and was hitched up over a waist girdle or belt. Instead of a wide neck opening some tunics had a smaller one provided with a vertical slit at the neck which facilitated putting it on and which might be closed by a pin or a brooch. The tunic might be decorated with embroidered bands at the cuff, neck or hem and occasionally the upper arm, where the band probably also served to hide the join between the sleeve and the main tunic. Simple all-over designs were also used. Some tunics were slit at the sides. A super-tunic might be worn over the tunic when the knight was not in armour. This was similar to the main tunic but sometimes a little shorter, and might have looser sleeves. On ceremonial occasions those of high rank might wear long tunics.

A rectangular or semicircular cloak of varying length provided extra warmth. It was fastened by ties or a brooch at the front or on the right shoulder to keep the arm free but cloaks were not usually worn when in armour. A purse (a pouch tied at the neck) might be carried under the tunic, suspended from the girdle which appeared at intervals from the braies. Gold or silver rings were worn and were also a sign of wealth, echoed in the quality of brooches or pins worn. The hair in the 10th century initially may have been long in Scandinavian style, perhaps worn in a heavy fringe. Some may latterly have copied the continental bowl crop round the tops of the ears. In the 11th century the back and sides were shaved in a distinctive fashion which can be seen on the Bayeux Tapestry but which did not last. Faces were usually clean shaven. In England during the reign of Rufus (1087–1100) very long hair and beards came into vogue, possibly helped by the longer hairstyle worn by the Anglo-Scandinavians.

The basic body defence of the Norman knight was the mailcoat. Mail consisted of numerous small iron rings each interlinked with four others to form a flexible defence. The coat so formed was pulled on over the head. Many of the first Normans would not have possessed any mail at all. Those who did would have had a coat which reached perhaps to the hip only and would be provided with short or elbow-length sleeves. During the first half of the 11th century there was a tendency for the coat to lengthen to knee length

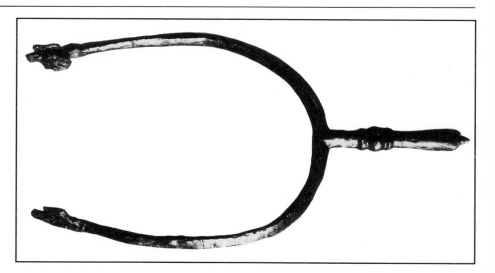

▶ *Tenth- and 11th-century prick spurs often terminated in a small point or points. The arms are always straight. The gilded spur of the knight is rarely borne out in finds of this period; many spurs are of iron, while those showing evidence of gilding are usually of copper-alloy. (By kind permission of Anthony de Reuck)*

▼ *A prick spur of the second half of the 11th century from Winchester castle, (Winchester Excavation Committee)*

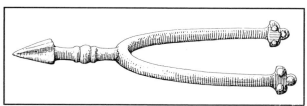

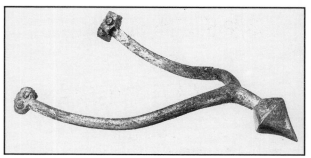

◀ *A Norman horseshoe of the 11th or 12th century. The wavy edge and countersunk holes are typical of the period. (By kind permission of Anthony de Reuck)*

▲ *A 12th- or 13th-century prick spur, showing the curved spur arm and angled shank. (By courtesy of the Board of Trustees, British Museum)*

forms of the mailcoat continued to be worn, rather by infantry than cavalry, throughout the century but the longer style had become usual by the time of the Norman Conquest.

Occasionally the neck of the mailcoat was extended to provide a protective hood or coif. This was the origin of the word associated with such a coat—*hauberk*—which came from the Old German word for a neck-guard—*hals berg*. Indeed a few hoods may have been made separately from the mailcoat but if this is so it was a fashion which did not last. Several shown on the Bayeux Tapestry lack any indication of rings which suggests they were of leather.

On the front of a number of hauberks seen on the Tapestry, worked within 20 years of the Battle of Hastings, several straps may be seen. Some are

or even just below the knees. In order to facilitate movement, and to allow a rider to sit his horse more easily, the skirts were usually slit up to the fork at the front and rear. When mounted, this allowed the skirt to hang naturally over the thigh at each side. Some of the earlier coats may still have been made with side vents, a fashion better suited to footsoldiers. Short

arranged as squares and some as horizontal lines at the neck, the latter also seen on mailcoats worn by the English. The exact function of such features are unknown. They are rarely seen outside the Bayeux Tapestry, only appearing on a few other contemporary illustrations. One theory is that they represent a loose flap of mail hanging down prior to being tied up over the throat and chin. This, the ventail, is certainly mentioned in the *Song of Roland* of about 1100. Moreover, just such a square is shown in the open and closed position on a mid 12th-century sculpted capital at Clermont Ferrand, France. A few figures on the Bayeux Tapestry do appear to have a flap drawn up in a similar manner to that on the capital. However, we are left to wonder whether those with only a single horizontal strap at the throat are supposed to have such a flap closed or whether they simply echo the edging straps which appear on many mailcoats on the tapestry. Again, the scene of hauberks being carried, together with some of the other sources, illustrate no mail hood to which such a flap would be tied, unless it is implied that it is hanging down loose at the rear. An alternative idea is that the square represents a loose mail flap tied over a vertical slit at the neck opening, which can be seen on other illustrations of such coats and was common on

*The Bayeux Tapestry was probably worked within 20 years of the Battle of Hastings. Here Count Guy of Ponthieu appears to wear a sleeveless coat of scale armour when receiving Duke William's messengers. (Bayeux Tapestry. With special permission of the town of Bayeux)*

civilian tunics. A third alternative, and perhaps the least likely, is that it represents a reinforcement of mail over the chest or even a plate beneath held by ties.

By the time of the Norman Conquest a few senior knights wore mail hose or chausses. These may have been simple strips of mail applied to the front of the leg and laced up the rear. Alternatively they may have been full hose, both styles braced up to the waist girdle of the braies. Since shoes are worn by such figures on the Bayeux Tapestry we cannot be sure whether the foot was protected, though it seems unlikely. Interestingly, a few knights wear mail on the forearms. Though one or two figures may have sleeves extended to the wrist, and while at least one French manuscript shows that such sleeves were known by this time, those shown largely appear to be separate from the elbow-length sleeves of the hauberk. They may have been made like the hose and slid up the arm. If so, it did not last as a fashion. Many knights on the Bayeux Tapestry have coloured bands up the forearm; this could be conceived as a conventional way of rendering the puckered sleeve often seen at this time if it was also seen on civilian costume, which it is not. It may represent some sort of leather strapping wound round the forearm for extra protection, or even perhaps some padded undergarment. Such banded sleeves are also shown on illustrations of English warriors.

The helmet of the time was conical and almost invariably made with a nasal or nose-guard. Some were almost certainly made like the old-fashioned *Spangenhelm*, in which vertical iron bands, usually four in number, spring from a brow-band and meet at the apex, the spaces between the bands being filled with iron segments riveted in place. Many helmets, however, seem to have been made from segments riveted directly to each other, whilst still others were beaten out of a single piece of metal. Though the nasal could be forged in one with the helmet, illustrations suggest that most were made with an applied brow-band. Additionally reinforcing bands might be added to these latter types. If the helmet was segmented the bands could cover the joints. Helmets might be painted, usually in the spaces between applied bands or else the segments themselves.

It is highly probable that all helmets were lined. As no lining and few helmets survive such ideas can only be hypotheses based on the presence of rivets and the examples of later helmets. It may be that a band of leather was riveted inside the brim, to which a coarse cloth lining was stitched, probably stuffed and quilted and possibly cut into segments which could be drawn together by a thong at the apex to adjust for height and comfort. The helmet would have been supplied with a tie at each side which fastened under the chin to secure it on the head. Contemporary

*Unarmoured riders attack the castle of Dol. As this picture follows a scene of marching it may represent knights galloping straight into action, one man having donned his helmet. However, it may also represent retainers or even perhaps squires. (Bayeux Tapestry. With special permission of the town of Bayeux)*

references to lacing helmets is common. It also helped prevent them from being knocked over the eyes.

The final item of armour for the knight was his shield. The first Normans would have carried a circular wooden shield, probably faced and perhaps lined with leather. A bar riveted vertically inside the shield allowed it to be carried and to accommodate the knuckles a hole was cut from the centre of the shield. In order to protect the exposed hand a conical metal boss was then riveted over the front. A longer strap allowed the shield to be hung in the hall or slung on the back; it also prevented loss in battle if dropped. A strop for the hand rather than a bar seems to have been used occassionally by c.1100, also being provided with an additional strap for the forearm. A pad to lessen the shock of blows may also have been provided. Although such additional strapping does not greatly assist in using such shields, some may have been added when carried by mounted men who might need to use the reins. Many shields are illustrated with an edging but surviving examples are very rare. Though such borders may simply have been painted, it seems likely that leather, iron or bronze strips may have been used to reinforce the edges. A number of illustrations suggest that some shields were additionally strengthened by bands springing from the central boss to the outer edge. Some are also shown as rather ovoid in shape but whether this reflects a true shape is open to question.

In about the year 1000 such shields were supplemented by the introduction of a new type, the so-called kite-shaped shield. In this form the lower edge of the circular shield was drawn down to a point, the resulting shape being similar to the old-fashioned kite. It has been said that this form was ideal for

*William confers arms on Earl Harold during his visit to Normandy, probably in 1064. The thick bands on the helmets suggest* spangenhelms. *The 'tails' on William's helmet are like the infulae on a bishop's mitre and may be a badge of rank, making him easy to spot from behind. The coifs do not appear to be of mail and are probably of leather. Notice the sword worn beneath the mail. (Bayeux Tapestry. With special permission of the town of Bayeux)*

horsemen, since the longer shape guarded the rider's left side and his vulnerable leg. However, such shields were initially seen in use equally by both cavalry and infantry. Moreover, many knights seem to carry their shields almost horizontally, as though attempting to protect their horse's left flank. The kite shield superseded the circular shield as the best type for cavalrymen, although the latter remained in use by some footsoldiers throughout the Middle Ages.

The carrying device on the new shield was no longer a metal bar. Instead there was an arrangement of straps, often a square or diamond (for hand and forearm) or else a saltire or single long strap for the hand, supplemented by others for the forearm. Now redundant, the boss remained as an ornamental feature on many shields right through into the 12th and occasionally the 13th century. Many of these shields were decorated, especially with wavy crosses and beasts such as two-legged dragons. These were not true heraldic symbols, since the same person is sometimes shown with two or three different devices. True heraldry was not to emerge until the 12th century.

The foregoing formed the basic equipment of the Norman knight until the 12th century. The mailcoat appears from illustrations to have been the most popular form of defence. However, other forms of protection may have been used on occasion. Coats of scale, in which small scales of horn, metal or even leather are attached to a canvas backing, had been known in western Europe since the Roman Empire. At least one seems to be shown on the Bayeux Tapestry. The less wealthy may have simply worn a coat of hide. Unfortunately, this is a poorly documented area. The 13th century St. Olaf's saga mentions coats of reindeer hide which could turn a blow as well as mail. One rider in a group of Norman horsemen on the Bayeux tapestry appears to wear a coat of brown material which is of identical cut to the mail hauberks around him. Lamellar, consisting of small metal plates laced together, may have been adapted by a few Italo-Norman knights.

It is possible that some form of padded garment was worn under the mail. The drawback with mail was its very flexibility, which allowed a heavy blow to break bones or cause severe bruising without actually tearing the links. Also, if links were broken they could be driven into a wound and cause blood poisoning. The form such garments took in the 10th and 11th centuries is likely to have been similar to that of the mailcoat. One or two garments seen on the Bayeux Tapestry may represent padded tunics but we cannot be sure. Even in the 13th century illustrations of mail being removed do not reveal the padding below. It is just possible that the bands shown at the edges of the hauberks in the Bayeux tapestry represent some padded lining, but this can only be supposition.

The weapon par excellence of the mounted knight was his sword. No other weapon was more esteemed or more celebrated and the girding on of a sword was the mark of knighthood. The type in use in the 10th century and into the 11th century was a double-edged cutting or slashing sword. It had a blade about 31 inches in length, tapering slightly

*A supply wagon is dragged down to the waiting ships ready to sail for England. It is unlikely that spears were barbed or had lugs in reality. The helmets are hooked over the uprights of the cart and appear to have solid neck-guards, though it may be meant to show the nasals of two helmets together. Each hauberk is carried on a pole by two men, since when not worn it represents dead weight. The coifs would hang down at the back. One sword is carried by a wrist strap. (Bayeux Tapestry. With special permission of the town of Bayeux)*

towards the point. Down the centre ran the fuller, not a blood channel but a method of lightening the blade without weakening it. Some men may have preferred an alternative but less common form which was longer with more parallel sides, the fuller being quite narrow. Sword hilts were fairly short, since the sword was meant to be used in one hand. The crossguard was often straight but might curve towards the blade slightly. The pommel, which helped to counterbalance the blade and also prevented the hand from sliding off the grip, was usually either shaped like a tea-cosy or like a brazil nut. More rarely a simple disc pommel might be seen.

The sword was sharp as a razor but both hard and flexible, being capable of a thrust if necessary. It was carried in a wooden scabbard often covered in leather and slung from the waist by a belt fastened with a buckle. In the 10th and early 11th century some may have been hung from a baldric over the right shoulder. The tip of the scabbard might have a chape to prevent scuffing, the mouth a locket. The scabbard might have occasionally been angled slightly back by joining it with a suspension strap to the side of the sword belt, in the manner seen on one or two Anglo-Saxon depictions of warriors. Occasionally the sword belt appears to have been worn under the mail, since many figures on the Bayeux Tapestry are shown wearing swords which have no visible means of support. This may be accidental, but several figures

are seen in which the scabbard itself is worn under the mail, the lower end protruding from the skirt or through a slit, the sword hilt similarly emerging from another slit at the hip.

The other main weapon of the knight was his lance. In the 10th and, to a lesser extent, the 11th century the lance was essentially a spear, a plain ash shaft fitted with an iron head of leaf or lozenge shape and with a fairly long socket. The Bayeux Tapestry shows mounted knights using their lances either to stab or to throw. Although the overarm illustration has been questioned as simply a stabbing action, at least one lance is shown in mid-air on the Bayeux Tapestry. In the 11th century the lance was also being 'couched' under the arm so that the full force of the rider and galloping horse was imparted to the tip. The lances of senior commanders might be fitted with a small pennon with tails which was nailed behind the head. One semicircular flag shown on the Bayeux Tapestry seems to have a raven depicted on it, a throwback to the pagan raven symbols of the Vikings.

Maces were far less commonly used than the sword, and appear to have consisted of a wooden haft fitted with an iron or bronze head moulded with pointed projections. One depicted on the Bayeux Tapestry suggests a flanged metal head, though this would be a very early date for this type. Senior commanders such as Duke William might carry a

*The warhorses poke their heads above the gunnels during the crossing. They are probably wearing halters as no bits are shown. (Bayeux Tapestry. With special permission of the town of Bayeux)*

*The motte is erected at Hastings. These artificial mounds topped with timber palisades and a wooden tower were quick to build. They were served by a bailey or courtyard protected by earthen bank and palisades. The whole castle would be surrounded by a ditch. Some castles consisted of a simple ringwork without a motte. Such structures continued in use thoughout our period. (Bayeux Tapestry. With special permission of the town of Bayeux)*

rough baton or 'baculum', presumably to signify their rank. This seems to be a descendant of the Roman centurion's vine rod. Of crude construction, it also stood out in battle from other maces. Axes were not popular with horsemen at this date, despite the Normans' Scandinavian descent.

The knight rode a warhorse or destrier, so-called perhaps because it was led on the right hand or itself led with the right leg. Destriers were specially selected and carefully bred. Consequently they were extremely expensive animals, costing at least eight times the price of a riding horse and often much more. Such mounts, as the Bayeux Tapestry makes graphically clear, were stallions whose natural aggression would be useful in a battle. Later medieval sources show that similar mounts were trained to lash out and kick and it cannot be ruled out that a similar desire lay behind the use of similar mounts by the Normans. These horses were probably similar in size to, or slightly smaller than, a heavy hunter and were most like the modern Andalusian. Indeed, William himself was sent gifts of horses by the King of Spain. The horse was deep-chested and muscular so that it had the required staying power yet was nimble enough to perform the necessary turns in battle.

Stallions required domination and their riders used curb bits and prick spurs fitted with simple spikes. The saddle had developed by the mid 11th century into a proper war saddle, provided with a raised pommel and cantle and long stirrups so that the knight was almost standing in the stirrups and rode straight-legged. This combination gave a sure seat in battle, braced his back in the charge with a levelled lance and helped him to keep his seat as he cut with his sword. To further brace his saddle it was provided with a breast band and in some cases a crupper band as well. By 1100 a knight might own an additional warhorse. He also needed a palfrey or riding horse and ideally a sumpter horse or mule for his baggage. The squire might ride the pack-horse or else a poorer-quality riding horse called a rouncy. All this equipment and horseflesh meant that knighthood was a very costly business.

### The 12th Century

As well as the tunic seen previously a new, close-fitting long version came into fashion, slit up at the front and sometimes worn with a girdle which might carry the sword. This version might have bell-shaped or pendulous cuffs which could be rolled back for action (1130s–1170s). Others had tight, turn-back ornamented cuffs. At the end of the century magyar sleeves, which gave a deep armhole, heralded the style of tunic of the next century. The braies shortened to the knees in mid century, becoming drawers. Long hose became popular, pulled up over

*The 12th century stone keep at Hedingham, Essex. The earliest examples date to the late 10th century in northern France and some were known in Normandy before the Conquest. They became commoner in the 12th century, sometimes provided with stone curtain walls.*

the drawers and made with a tongue at the upper front edge by which it was fastened with a tie to an exposed portion of the braies girdle. Hair remained long, parted in the middle and accompanied by beard and moustache. Younger men were often clean shaven with hair to the nape only. According to Orderic Vitalis, one method of distinguishing knight from squires in the time of Henry I was by the shorter hairstyle worn by the latter who were not allowed to grow their locks. Following the battle of Bourgthéroulde William Lovel escaped disguised as a squire after cutting his hair.

The mailcoat of the 11th century could be seen throughout the 12th century and indeed into the next century. However, many representations show certain developments. The length remained at or just below the knee although some longer versions are seen occasionally. The sleeves now tended to extend to the wrists and towards the end of the century these had further developed into mail mittens. A half-way style can be seen on an illumination of Joshua in the Winchester Bible of 1160–70, where several figures have the hand covered in mail but the fingers left exposed. Once the whole hand was covered in mail a leather or cloth palm was necessary to allow for grip; since the sleeve and mitten were made in one, a slit in the palm enabled the hand to be freed as necessary. Often a lace was threaded through the links at the wrist and tied to prevent the mail sleeve dragging down onto the hand.

By the end of the century a quilted cap, similar to the civilian coif in shape, can be seen worn beneath the mail hood. Very occasionally a separate mail hood is shown but most were made in one with the mailcoat. Now the ventail flap is seen more often. Rectangular versions have been mentioned in connection with the capital at Clermont Ferrand, one such covering the face up to the eyes. Other ventails took the form of a pendulous flap which was drawn up across the throat and chin to be secured to the mail coif at the temple by a lace. Some appear to have consisted of a simple lace used to close a vertical slit in the mail protecting the throat. Mail chausses became increasingly popular, though still occasionally worn with shoes. Some chausses had a lace threaded through the links below the knee to help keep them in place.

Many 12th-century illustrations show knights with a long undergarment flowing from below the mail skirt. It has been suggested that this is a padded gambeson but the form seems too loose for such a garment. Moreover, although in mid century Wace mentions gambesons as an alternative to mail and though padded coats appear in the 1181 Assize of Arms and in conjunction with mailcoats in a description of the 3rd Crusade, these are references to infantrymen. The first descriptions of padding worn below the mail appear in the early 13th century. Although this does not negate the suggestion that such garments were worn earlier, it cannot as yet be proven. It may well be that these skirts are in fact the long gowns which have already been referred to as becoming popular in the 12th century.

By mid century a new garment had appeared: the surcoat. This was worn over the mailcoat. A few illustrations show long sleeves and pendulous cuffs (again reminiscent of civilian fashion) but the majority were sleeveless and split up the fork at front and

rear. For this reason it is rather hard to believe the idea put forward in one 14th-century chronicle that the surcoat kept the armour clean and dry. It may well have proved of some use during the crusades to fend off the heat of the sun from the metal links. It is just as likely, however, that its origins lay in a desire to emulate the long flowing garments worn by the Saracens. Most surcoats were tied at the waist with a girdle or belt which was separate from that securing the sword. Early surcoats were often white or self-coloured and perhaps had a contrasting lining. Some were soon used for decorative display, although this was not necessarily heraldic. Heraldry was a very new science with rules of usage. One man ought to have one coat of arms only, which passed to his eldest son on his death. Rules also governed the use of colour on colour. Surcoats were not greatly used for heraldic display until the 14th century.

Scale hauberks continued in use. Wace refers to another garment, the curie, which, as its name implies, was probably of leather. Unfortunately no 12th-century representation seems to exist but 13th-century sources suggest it was a waist-length garment put on over the head and tied or buckled at the sides. It may even have been reinforced with iron. Some are

*During the 12th century some palisades on the motte were replaced by stone walls to form a shell keep, though only a few stone towers were built on the mounds because of the weight. Several castles appeared with no motte or keep, relying on a strong stone curtain wall.*

worn by knights over mail but under surcoats, others without other armour by infantrymen.

The conical helmet with nasal remained throughout the 12th century but variations appeared early. Many now had the apex tilted forward whilst some were drawn down at the rear to form a neck-guard. During the second half of the century hemispherical forms and, from about 1180, cylindrical types appeared, with or without nasals. Also at this time a few German illustrations show a bar appearing on the end of the nasal to protect the mouth. By the end of the century this had developed into a full face guard, provided with two slits for the eyes and pierced with ventilation holes or slots to assist breathing. The cylindrical form was a popular type for this new development. Used in conjunction with a neck-guard, this new helmet foreshadows the great helm of the 13th century. That of Richard I has a tall fan crest, presumably of metal, on which a lion passant guardant is painted, echoing those on his shield.

Other helmets might also be painted, though not all such decoration carried heraldic significance.

In addition, a new form of helmet, the kettle hat, made its appearance in mid century. The Scandinavian chesspieces from the Isle of Lewis in Scotland suggest that two forms were in use: one had a cylindrical top with a deep angled brim; the other was very like the 20th-century tin hat. Primarily a footsoldier's helmet, we know from 13th-century sources that occasionally knights wore the kettle hat in preference to the stuffy helm, a situation which may have been met with in the late 12th century also.

The kite-shaped shield continued throughout the 12th century. However, by the 1150s many shields began to have the top edge cut straight, allowing the

knight to peer over without the sides curving down away from him as they did on the 11th-century form. Many shields were curved to the wearer's body. By the end of the century the length of some shields had slightly reduced. Shield bosses continued in a decorative function for example the newly discovered conical boss from the castle at Repton.

The double-edged cutting sword described earlier remained the main knightly weapon. Towards the end of the century a new type with a slightly tapered blade and shorter fuller emerged and became the most popular style of the next century. Alternative pommels also appeared. One was shaped like a lozenge and was fashionable after about 1175. Swords were still often worn beneath the mailcoat. Others show the popular method of fastening; the longer end of the belt was slit into two tails which were passed through two slits cut in the other end and knotted together.

As well as pennons similar to those seen on the Bayeux Tapestry, some triangular types were also used. Wace distinguishes between the gonfalon of the baron and the pennon of the knight. A number of

*A squadron of knights rides towards the battlefield at Hastings. One man does not wear mail but appears in an identical coat coloured in brown thread, possibly meant to represent hide. All except this figure have squares on their chests; those galloping to their right do not, suggesting ventails which have then been laced up. (Bayeux Tapestry. With special permission of the town of Bayeux)*

bronze polygonal mace heads have survived which may date to the 12th century. Though light in comparison to later versions, they would be capable of disabling an unarmoured man or cause damage through flexible mail.

By the later 12th century the knightly saddle had developed the front and rear boards or arçons so that the rear arçon curved round the knight's thighs and that at the front also curved. A long saddle cloth, sometimes with a dagged lower edge, was sometimes laid over the saddle, the arçons passing through slits in the cloth.

# CONSTRUCTION AND REPAIR

Little contemporary mail has survived, although the so-called mailcoat of St Wenceslas at Prague may be of 10th century date and a rolled mailcoat, probably from the battlefield of Lena in 1208, is preserved in Stockholm. Later medieval shirts show that mail weighed approximately 30 lbs. Most of the weight was taken on the shoulders but the drag could be reduced by hitching the mail over a waist or sword belt.

A mailcoat was the end product of a process which took many hours of labour. The exact method of making mail in the medieval period is unknown but scraps of information plus intelligent guesswork have arrived at a not improbable method of construction. The links began as drawn iron wire which was wound round a rod. The links so formed were then separated by being cut down one side of the rod. This left a number of open-ended rings. The ends of each ring were then hammered flat, overlapped and pierced in readiness to receive a tiny iron rivet. Every ring was interlinked with four others, two above and two below and then riveted shut. Since only every other row of rings needed to be riveted in order to join the rows above and below, the other rows could be welded shut. However, surviving medieval mail usually consists of wholly riveted rings. An 'idle' ring was only linked with three others and so could be used to decrease the number of rings in a row or the number of rows, so allowing a garment to be shaped. Thus a small hole under the armpit prevented the links from bunching up. The mail garment was designed with the rivet heads on the outside so that they did not rub against the clothing underneath and so wear it and themselves away. It is possible that certain tools were in use which overlapped, flattened

*The knights are supported by archers clad in tunics except for one man who may be an officer. (Bayeux Tapestry. With special permission of the town of Bayeux)*

At the disaster at the hillock, one knight strikes overarm while another thrusts with his lance couched under the arm. The scene shows how panic and boggy ground can affect even drilled horsemen. (Bayeux Tapestry. With special permission of the town of Bayeux)

and pierced each link in one movement but this can only be hypothesis. It is likely that the mailmaker actually made up the garments, leaving the more repetitious work of producing the links to his apprentices.

Scale armour would be made by riveting the upper edge of each scale to a leather or canvas backing garment and overlapping downwards so the top of the next scale was thus covered. Padded garments would have consisted of two layers of cloth or canvas stuffed with wool, hay, hair, old cloth or tow and quilted, usually vertically but perhaps also in a diamond pattern, to keep the stuffing in place.

Helmets were made in several ways. In order to make a segmented helmet each segment, usually four in number, had to be shaped, overlapped and riveted together. Those made from one piece were drawn up from a flat piece of iron hammered out over a shaped iron stake secured in a hole in the anvil. The steel was annealed, that is heated and cooled, to make it workable. Once formed, applied bands, neck-guards or face-guards were riveted on. In the case of *spangenhelm* the iron framework was forged and fitted together before the segments were fixed inside with rivets. Internal linings would be secured with rivets along the brim.

Many shields were made from several planks of wood glued side by side. It may be that some—circular rather than kite-shaped—were of laminated form, that is of perhaps two layers, each of which was placed with the grain running at right-angles to its neighbours for added strength. Some kite-shaped shields may have been formed from a single piece of wood. The earliest surviving shield is not Norman but belonged to the von Brienze family. It may date to the late 12th or early 13th century, although its rounded top was cut flat at some time between 1230 and 1250. It is 15 mm thick and may originally have been 100 cm long, being covered in parchment on both sides. Most shields were probably made from lime wood or possibly poplar. The dished appearance of some circular shields and the curved surface of many long shields was probably achieved through steam heating. Leather, when used, would be tacked at the edges on the rim or at the rear. Enarmes and guige were riveted through the wood, the heads visible on the outer face. Bosses were similarly riveted through to the rear.

The sword had undergone a change of manufacture. Until about 900, sword blades were produced by pattern-welding. Since a good blade was handed down and since the knife known as the seax, together with spear heads, continued to be pattern-welded until after the Norman Conquest, a description of the technique is called for. Rods of iron and carburised iron (a soft, impure form of steel) were beaten and twisted together to form a sandwich which was then twisted with similar sandwiches to form the blade, hammered out and flattened and shaped. The twisting of the metals meant that when the blade was finished and polished, a wavy line was seen running down its length, the pattern.

By about 900, however, improvements in the forging of steel meant that new types of sword could now be made. In order to harden the steel it was first quenched to temper the metal. The very hardness, however, gave this steel a brittleness which the older iron and carburised iron had not possessed. It was therefore necessary to employ the steel in such a way that the sword did not shatter easily. In order to achieve this the smiths used the steel in various combinations with the more malleable iron to produce harder but flexible blades. Some swords had tough steel edges welded on to improve their sharpness. It is impossible to know which methods were favoured the most, since different smiths favoured different combinations. Some felt that honey was a better medium for quenching because it created less bubbles. Similarly, the reaction of quenching could differ from sword to sword within the same smithy. Moreover, many surviving swords have not been analysed at all.

Sword blades might be decorated. Grooves were cut into the blade and the decoration was hammered into the heated surface. On the other side another design might spell a name such as 'ULFBERHT' in Roman letters. Other names were also used, especially at this time: 'INGELRII'. These were probably originally the names of swordsmiths, but by the time of the Conquest they had come to denote the factory. Many seem to have been based in the Rhineland, from whence swords were sent to their customers.

The most common smith's name when set into the narrow fullers of the longer swords and their derivatives was: 'GICELIN ME FECIT'. On the reverse, especially of the latter, might be found a religious inscription, usually 'INNOMINIDOMINI' or a garbled version of it. Other metals were also used for decoration: latten (which was a type of brass), silver, pewter or tin. Well-written religious phrases in latten or white metal were especially seen, some misspelt or obscure, usually on the long swords or their derivatives. Crosses might flank an inscription. Rarer decoration came in the form of symbolic pictographs and mystical designs.

The metal crossguard was slotted on to the tang and secured by the grip. This was formed from two pieces of wood or horn channelled out to take the

*Bishop Odo, who probably did not participate in the actual fighting, rallies the 'puers' or boys who are not yet knights. The word itself may be a reworking; if accurate, it shows that at this date young men training for knighthood were allowed to wear full armour and to fight. Odo may be wearing some sort of quilted garment. (Bayeux Tapestry. With special permission of the town of Bayeux)*

metal tang, then glued over it and probably covered in leather and perhaps bound with thongs. The pommel was slotted over the end of the tang which was then hammered over to secure it.

The repair of a knight's equipment in the field depended on what was damaged and whether a smith or armourer was on hand. In the invasion of England there would be a number of armourers travelling with the host. For small-scale skirmishing it is doubtful whether a skilled technician would be available until the knight returned to his home base or reached another castle.

Mail might tear but still render the garment usable until such time as it could be repaired. It is doubtful if a village smithy would have the type of tools required for the tiny holes and rivets needed to close up links. He could probably beat out a dented helmet, however, until a more skilled repair could be effected by an armourer. Rents in cloth were probably stitched up by squires or, when an army was on the march, by some of the women that accompanied it. Shields, although tough, were not designed for long usage. Viking sagas note the effects of sharp weapons against shields during formal duels, when the wood was hacked to pieces leaving only the metal bosses intact. Damaged shields would be discarded rather than repaired, only the boss and perhaps any metal fittings or straps being salvaged. Swords were prized items and only an armourer could deal with damage, though again a blacksmith could straighten out a bent weapon temporarily if no swordsmith was to hand.

Whilst speaking of repair it is perhaps worth

*William raises his helmet to scotch rumours of his death at the crisis of the battle. He seems to wear separate mail sleeves on the forearms. The angle of the helmet suggests it is actually held by its chin straps. On Eustace of Boulogne the square on the chest is visible, as if the ventail has been loosened to aid identification. (Bayeux Tapestry. With special permission of the town of Bayeux)*

noting the kind of services available to the knight himself should he be wounded. Good care was probably given by monks, who used numerous herbs in their healing. However, a knight was likely to receive the attention of surgeons if in an army or of great rank, or of lesser men if himself of humbler rank. Knights in southern Italy might be lucky enough to be tended by men trained at the great school of Salerno. Head wounds were less common in knights because they usually wore helmets but were more likely to suffer dislocated shoulders from falling off their horses. Such wounds were frequently treated by placing a ball covered in wool under the arm and forcing the joint back. Throat wounds, often from a lance, were usually considered untreatable. Wounds were often left partially open for a day or two until pus formed, before stitching up. The more enlightened used egg white and other remedies as opposed to boiling oil or hot cautery irons found elsewhere. Amputation might be done with an axe but suturing of blood vessels was known. Barbed arrows were removed either by covering the barb with a tube or quill, or by pushing them through to the other side and breaking off the head before withdrawing the shaft.

# TRAINING

The actual training of the Norman knight is little documented. Indeed, references to squires tend to suggest that while some boys of good birth were so-called, a much higher proportion were in fact non-noble attendants who would never attain knighthood and who were paid—often erratically—for the job they performed. From 11th- and 12th-century ac-

**St Benedict frees a prisoner,** *a manuscript of c.1070 from Monte Cassino in Italy. This is one of the rare chances to see a saddle from the front and shows a rounded bow similar in shape to a southern French picture which shows a cantle. (Ms. Lat. 1202, Vatican Lib., Rome)*

An Italian ivory chessman, probably of the 11th century. He may be wearing a short lamellar coat and has a kite-shaped shield whose lattice pattern suggests reinforcing iron strips. The head may be protected by a leather coif or even a stylised helmet. A footsoldier figure from the same group has a helmet with nasal which appears to be extended down over the ears and neck, although this may be intended to depict helmet and coif. (Cabinet des Medailles, Bibliothèque Nationale, Paris)

counts and from the more detailed rule of the Knights Templar of the 13th century a picture of these duties may be formed.

The squire was often heavily laden, carrying his own and his master's pack and weapons. According to the Rule, he rode either the pack-horse or a rouncy and led his master's saddled war-horse. In the battle line he took the riding-horse to the rear after giving the knight his shield and lance. If a spare war-horse was owned, a second squire followed his master at a safe distance, ready to assist if the first horse was killed or blown.

When on campaign the squire set up the knight's tent before riding out to forage for firewood and

*A second chessman may be intended to be wearing a sleeved long mailcoat rather than lamella. Some Italo-Norman horsemen may have adopted the armour they encountered in Italy. (Cabinet des Medailles, Bibliothèque, Nationale, Paris)*

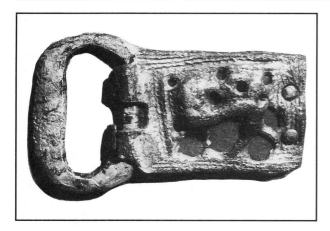

*Eleventh- and 12th-century buckles. Clockwise: Gilt copper-alloy buckle, 10th–11th century; enamelled bezel, 11th century; gilt copper-alloy buckle, 11th–12th century; buckle recessed for enamel, 12th–13th century; gilt copper-alloy buckle, 12th–13th century; iron buckle, perhaps from horse's girth strap, 1200–1250. (By kind permission of Anthony de Reuck)*

water, especially for the horses. Squires often seem to have set out in groups, sometimes with an armed escort. They were also prominent in sieges and when a place was sacked. Young men of good birth were more likely to be the ones who helped a knight dress and put on his armour, or who carved at the table. They also may have worn armour and fought, as suggested by a reference on the Bayeux Tapestry.

It is obvious that a professional cavalryman must work hard to acquaint himself not only with the niceties of riding with minimal hand control but also with the use of the lance and sword from horseback. According to Abbot Suger in the early 12th century, a boy (or 'puer') destined for knighthood was placed in the household of another lord when about 12 or 13 years old. Thus William Marshal was placed in the household of his uncle, William of Tancarville, in 1155. Such a move might be easier for some than for others since some lords, such as Henry I, were actively on the lookout for new young blood to join their ranks and had the money to support their training. Lords who could not place their sons in the household of the king of a great magnate did the best they could.

Boys were taught to ride at an early age. The Carolingian comment: 'You can make a horseman of a lad at puberty, after that, never', was echoed by the remark: 'He who has stayed at school till the age of twelve, and never ridden a horse, is fit only to be a priest.' The boisterous stallions were not easy to control, which explains somewhat the use of a harsh bit and prick spurs. Boys therefore had to learn to master these wilful animals as well as to ride with their legs, allowing their hands to concentrate on using the shield in the left hand and the weapon in the right. The left hand is sometimes shown holding the rein as well but close combat would mean either laying the rein on the horse's neck or else keeping the shield fairly still.

It took much practice to be a good fighter. References occasionally occur, such as that of the knight accidentally killed while practising the javelin with his squire. Thirteenth- and 14th-century illustrations show how warriors trained at the pell, a tall wooden post driven into the ground at which they could practise their sword cuts. Later medieval texts, following Roman manuals, describe training weapons as being of double weight to develop the muscles.

Once the lance began to be couched under the arm it became necessary to learn how to stay in the saddle under the shock of impact and how to grip the lance firmly so that it did not slide back under the armpit when contact was made. The lance of the Norman knight had no ring behind the hand to ram against the armpit and prevent friction burns.

There is no reason to think that trainee knights did not practise in the same way as is shown in 14th-century manuscripts. This involved early training by use of a wheeled wooden horse pulled by companions. The pupil aimed at a shield nailed to a post and, once struck, the wooden horse continued to be pulled to teach the youth to grip firmly with his legs and to hold on to the lance, so preventing either loss of the weapon or an ignominious unseating. The same target could be challenged when riding a warhorse. As well as inanimate opponents, apprentice knights could fight each other or another knight, to learn not only the basic cuts but also feints and the offensive use of the shield.

The 'puer' was dubbed a knight when about twenty-one years old, a translation initially made by a stout buffet about the ears, the only blow the young man would have to receive without retaliating. The ceremony was performed by another knight, usually the lord of the household but sometimes the king himself. The new knight's sword was belted round him and his spurs buckled to his feet. He then showed off his prowess, sometimes in a celebratory tournament.

As a new member of an elite equestrian society the young man was now known as a youth ('juvenis') and remained so until he settled down, married and had children, after which he was referred to in written texts as a man ('vir'). Since some knights, such as William Marshal, did not marry until they were into middle age, their years as a youth could last for some time. They maintained their training by riding at dummy targets and practising skill at arms with other knights or boys.

It was youths, as knights errant, who rode out to seek fame, money, wives, or positions. They took service with lords, sometimes in far-flung lands, either as mercenaries or as household knights and flocked to theatres of war. Those younger sons with little prospect of a part of the patrimony were on the lookout for a rich heiress who could provide them with land. They took part in tournaments which were emerging in the 11th century and which were established during the next century. Here was an excellent training ground. The tournament of the day consisted of a battle between two teams of knights wearing full armour and using unblunted weapons. The field might stretch over a large area of the countryside and contestants had every incentive to fight hard since defeated knights forfeited their horse and armour. Thus good fighters such as William Marshal stood to make a fortune and toured events looking for gain and glory.

As men of action, Norman knights were perfectly attuned to the hunt. It supplied additional food for the table but also provided the chance to improve horsemanship by galloping after game over rough country. Certainly it could be dangerous; Richard, son of William the Conqueror, is said to have been gored to death by a stag in the New Forest, which his father had created. Accidents were common and not all caused by the enraged quarry. The same forest witnessed the death of another of the Conqueror's sons, William Rufus, killed by an arrow which some have tried to suggest was the result of an assassination plot by his brother, Henry. Against wild boar or rarely the brown bear, the hunt provided the chance to demonstrate courage in tackling such animals with sword or spear. Moreover, the hunting field was the one place where the knight might show his skill with the bow or crossbow.

# TACTICS

The Norman knight was the shock element in the armies of the day. Initially cavalry battles are poorly documented but probably consisted of groups of horsemen, each under its lord's gonfanon, galloping against the enemy. Such groups or 'conrois', comprising perhaps 25 or 50 men, may have used their lances in various ways; certainly the Bayeux Tapestry shows little co-ordination of movements and couching the lance is not a priority. It was probably not

*The Norman kings of England changed the style of seal used by their Anglo-Saxon predecessors in order to show themselves as warrior knights riding their warhorses. This is the great seal of Henry I (1100–1135). Equipment shows little change to that of 1066 except for long sleeves to the mailcoat. (Public Records Office, London)*

*The south door of the cathedral at Bari in southern Italy possesses early 12th-century carvings which portray mailed knights wearing armour similar in style to that seen used by the Normans elsewhere. The left-hand figure appears to be about to throw his lance or strike overarm. (By kind permission of Dr David Nicolle)*

until the late 11th century that couching the lance became usual, so that Anna Comnena speaks of the knight of the 1st Crusade being able to punch a hole in the walls of Babylon. This method enabled conrois to charge in a solid line, knee to knee and so close that it was said of one group of feudal knights in the 3rd Crusade that an apple thrown into their midst would not have touched the ground.

The initial charge with the couched lance was begun at a trot, only breaking into a gallop at the last moment so as not to tire the horses or lose formation. Similarly the lance was held upright at the start and only levelled on nearing the enemy. The idea was to drive the iron into an opponent or else to unseat him or overthrow both horse and rider. For this the man or his shield must be hit squarely and the lance gripped firmly and kept clamped under the arm. Late medieval tournament books advise not looking at the oncoming lance point as this will make you flinch or close your eyes; instead you should concentrate on the oncoming target. The charge was followed up by drawing the secondary weapons and raining blows. The tournament books suggest that in the mêlée in the lists the knight should strike and press on to the next, not turning round as this wastes time and becomes tiring—advice likely to apply equally to earlier centuries.

The initial charge was important for, if it could be held, the attack might peter out. To this end the Byzantines, uncomfortable when facing Norman cavalry, would sometimes try to break them up by throwing down caltrops to maim the horses or else by using light wagons as an obstacle. Against solid infantry the mounted knight was more at a disadvantage. Here the use of volleys of javelins, delivered by groups of horsemen who then wheeled away, are possibly suggested by the Bayeux Tapestry. Such tactics were probably copied from the Bretons and against a phalanx of infantry may have proved more useful than a charge with couched lances. Any weak spots so caused could then be exploited by groups of knights bursting in with drawn swords. In either case the knight was soon reduced to a long contest of hard knocks with secondary weapons where his stamina and strength would be tested to the limit.

Although he could fight on foot, Anna Comnena noted that the long shield and spurs seemed to be a disadvantage for the dismounted knight. However, against both foot and horse he could employ the trick of the feigned flight to lure them out. This manoeuvre has been the subject of much controversy. The usual argument has been that it would panic the rest of the army, or that the enemy would guess what was afoot. It is simply the chronicler's way of covering up a real retreat, say the critics. It was especially suited to the conrois, since one or more such units could be

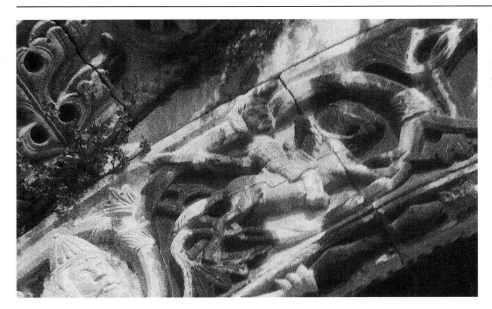

*A bare-headed figure on the west front of Bari cathedral may be wearing a coat of scale. (By kind permission of Dr David Nicolle)*

employed. Many fought with the companions they knew and trained with, thus a feeling of camaraderie and fellow-thinking could be utilised to reduce possible confusion. Moreover, feigned flights had been a part of cavalry tactics for centuries. Certainly the Bretons had been using them since the 9th century and it is possible that the Normans were influenced by the latter. Norman knights are recorded as using feigned flights to great effect at Arques in 1053 and Cassel in 1071. They also used this tactic in Sicily, at Messina, in 1060.

Enemy arrows were a problem since the warhorse was unarmoured and his rider's limbs and face were partly exposed. Here it was necessary to avoid a head-on confrontation and to try to take the enemy in the flank. When faced with eastern horse archers the heavier horses and the solid charge of the mailed knights could do little against enemies who refused to stand and, mounted on swift horses, harassed the westerners with arrows, particularly on the flanks. It meant that such enemies had to be forced into a position from which the charge could be launched, or ambushed to allow the knights to close quickly. Bohemond formed a reserve of mounted knights in an attempt to counter flank attacks on his charging knights. He also made good use of his infantry to form a screen behind which the cavalry could wait for an opportune moment to deliver their charge. The armoured spearmen could in their turn cover the archers and crossbowmen who could keep their

enemies at a distance. In this way each arm of the army complemented the others and provided an effective counter-measure.

It might be thought that Normans who broke through and pursued a defeated enemy would be difficult to rally. The fact that they could be halted, even when individuals used their lances in different ways rather than in a concerted charge, testifies to the discipline and order seen on the field.

# TYPICAL ENGAGEMENTS

The effectiveness of the Norman cavalry charge, with or without the couched lance, is demonstrated in a number of battles. Val-és-Dunes in 1047 was a struggle between Duke William of Normandy and a force of Norman rebels. There is little reference to the presence of infantry and it appears to have largely involved clashes of bodies of horsemen in which the stronger or more skilful, under William and King Henry, won the day. Even against mixed forces the power of a Norman assault could be decisive. In 1081 at Durazzo an Italo-Norman charge broke the Byzantine line which included horse archers. At Monte Maggiore in 1041, about 2,000 Normans in revolt against their Byzantine masters faced a larger army drawn up in two lines. The Norman horse and foot attacked in spearhead formation—presumably a kind of wedge—and drove the first line in on the second, causing confusion and ultimate defeat. In 1053 the battle of Civitate again saw Norman knights, this time from Apulia, quickly routing a larger Papal force of Italo-Lombard cavalry and infantry in the first charge. However, the Norman knights under Humphrey de Hauteville and their reserve under Robert Guiscard were held up by a group of about 700 Swabian mercenaries until Richard's horsemen returned from the pursuit and forced them into squares which were gradually dissipated.

Hard pounding was used far more at Hastings in 1066. According to William of Poitiers, the lines of the Normans and their allies consisted of archers in front, infantry behind and knights in rear. This strongly suggests an initial softening up with missiles, followed with an assault by the foot. The cavalry were to be used to break open the gaps so formed and to pursue the routed enemy. Such tactics made sense. For one thing, the Normans probably had fewer horsemen than they would have liked and were confronted by a solid dismounted phalanx. Secondly, warhorses were expensive and were more likely to be killed by footsoldiers than by other mounted knights. Moreover, as we shall see, this combination of elements in Norman armies was usual. In reality, the Norman foot at Hastings was unable to effect breaches and the cavalry were committed in a desperate attempt to break the English line, made more secure by being positioned on a ridge which denied flank attack. Victory was only achieved towards evening when a combination of mixed cavalry and infantry assaults and arrow showers finally saw King Harold killed. The English position had shrunk so much that the ends of the ridge were seized by cavalry who then rolled up the line.

The ferocity of English resistance was not lost on the Normans. It must have reinforced their belief, shared by other feudal commanders in Europe, that dismounted knights were often tactically desirable. Indeed, Norman forces often appear to have dismounted a part of their cavalry while keeping others as a mounted reserve. Moreover, archers were usually placed in front so that the resulting army consisted of similar elements to those at Hastings, although the shortage of cavalry here meant that the infantry consisted of footsoldiers, knights only joining them when their horses had been killed.

The tactic of dismounting some of his knights to form a solid defence supported by horsemen won the day for Henry I on several occasions. In 1106 he was besieging Tinchebrai when his brother arrived with a relief force. Instead of backing off, Henry chose to fight. He placed his infantry in the front line and

*The two knights on the right in this frieze from the south door at Bari appear to wear coats of lamella, slightly obscured by their kite-shaped shields. (By kind permission of Dr David Nicolle)*

*Goliath is shown as a warrior with an enormous shield in the Bible of St Etienne, a northern French manuscript of 1109–11. Notice the saltire arrangement of the straps for the hand grip, and the long guige strap round the neck. (Bib. Munic., Dijon, Ms 168, f.5r)*

dismounted knights in the second, with a contingent of 700 cavalry with each. Robert apparently also dismounted some of his forces. He then launched a cavalry charge against Henry's right wing, Henry of Huntingdon noted that they had been well trained in the wars of Jerusalem, probably a reference to the solid charge with couched lances. It broke through Henry's first line but was held by the second, a similar charge on the left wing making little progress. However, Henry then sent a hidden reserve of perhaps 1,000 cavalry under Helias of Maine against the entangled Normans on his right and won the day. At Brémule in 1119 Henry dismounted all but about 100 of his 500 knights when he encountered the invading forces of Louis VI of France. It was a small-scale affair since Louis himself had only about 400 knights. The French came on in two or three divisions and the first, though apparently lacking discipline, actually broke the Norman cavalry screen. However, on confronting the dismounted knights it

was surrounded and cut to pieces, as was the next division. Louis, himself wounded in the head, fled.

At the Battle of the Standard near Northallerton in 1138 knights fought on foot to stiffen the English levies against the opposing Scots. Again archers completely disrupted the undisciplined Galwegian charge and, though the Norman cavalry of David of Scotland had some success, they were withstood probably by the Norman mounted contingent fighting for Stephen. At Lincoln in 1141 both King Stephen and the rebel forces placed wings of horsemen on either side of a centre of infantry and dismounted knights.

The danger in attacking archers is well illustrated by the Battle of Bourgthéroulde in 1124. This battle is important, not so much for the historical outcome—no king was present—as for the concise tactical description given by Orderic Vitalis. Henry I's household knights confronted the rebel Waleran of Meulan who was returning from an attempt to relieve Vatteville. After discussion the royal troops decided to dismount one section and support it with the other which remained mounted. A screen of archers was placed in front to shoot down the enemy horses. Mounted archers, who almost certainly only used their horses for movement, were sent against Waleran's right wing. His knights had their mounts shot from under them and Waleran was captured. Henry was on the receiving end when attempting to relieve Alençon in 1118, however. Angevin archers in a second force advanced and took their toll of the royal troops; a charge by Count Fulk from the siege lines then broke Henry's forces.

One way to entice infantry to break their line was the feigned flight. At Hastings the fleeing cavalry easily outstripped their infantry pursuers and were able to recover and turn on them. The manoeuvres could have been pre-arranged during a lull when groups of cavalry were gathered on the valley floor.

Flank attacks have already been noted in the sudden onslaught of cavalry used by Henry I at Tinchebrai. At Nocera in 1132 the rebel, Rainulf of Avelino, secured victory over Roger II of Sicily by wheeling his force of 2,500 Apulian Norman horsemen against the flank of the Sicilian forces who had pushed back the rebel left wing. Several references occur of knights ambushing enemies. In 1119 the Norman garrison of Tillières, by keeping the paths

**Grip**

**Boss**

Early knight, c.1000
1: *Spangenhelm*, early 11th century
2: Circular shield, late 10th century

**A**

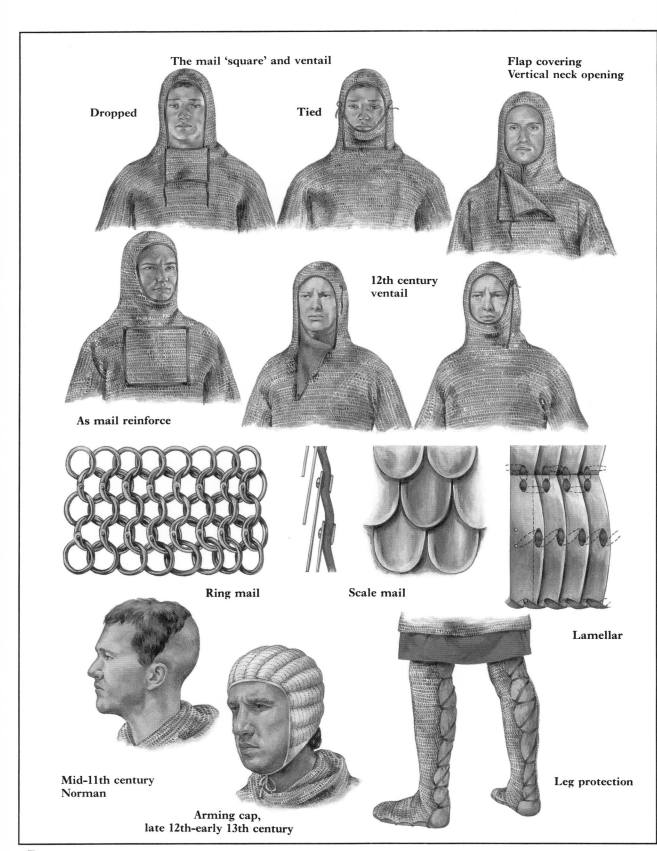

The mail 'square' and ventail

Dropped

Tied

Flap covering
Vertical neck opening

As mail reinforce

12th century
ventail

Ring mail

Scale mail

Lamellar

Mid-11th century
Norman

Arming cap,
late 12th-early 13th century

Leg protection

B

1: Norman Knight, c. 1066
2: Segmented helmet, mid-11th century

C

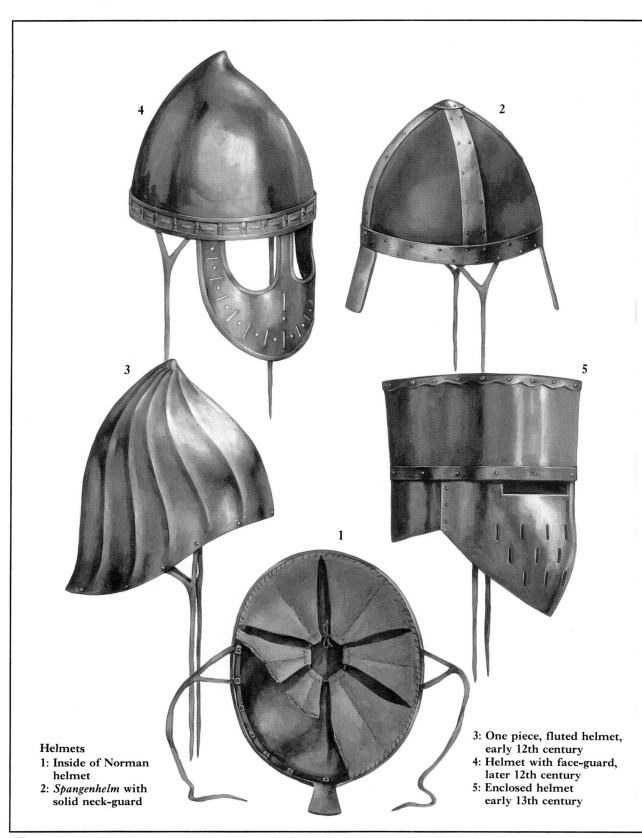

**Helmets**

**1:** Inside of Norman helmet

**2:** *Spangenhelm* with solid neck-guard

**3:** One piece, fluted helmet, early 12th century

**4:** Helmet with face-guard, later 12th century

**5:** Enclosed helmet early 13th century

D

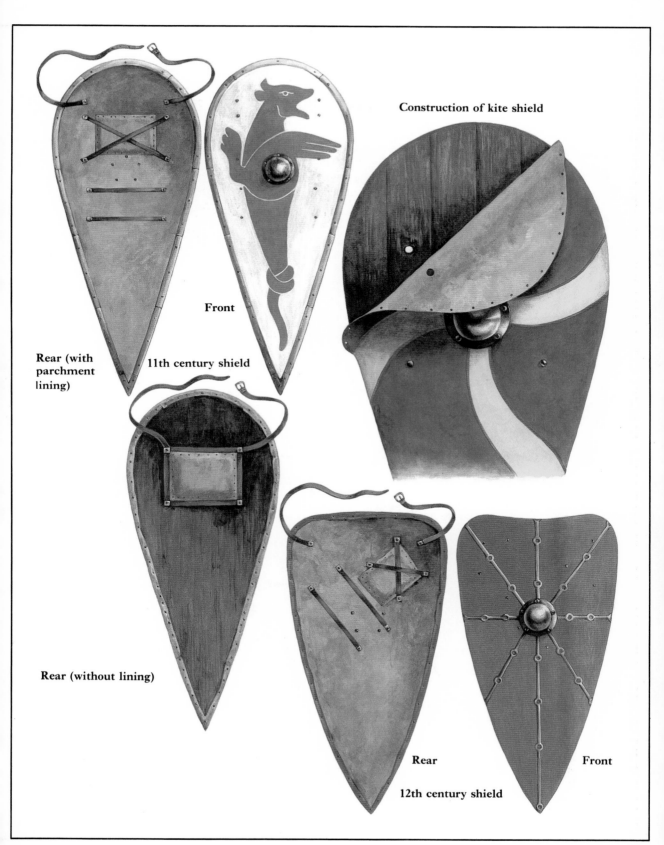

Rear (with parchment lining)

Front

11th century shield

Construction of kite shield

Rear (without lining)

Rear

Front

12th century shield

E

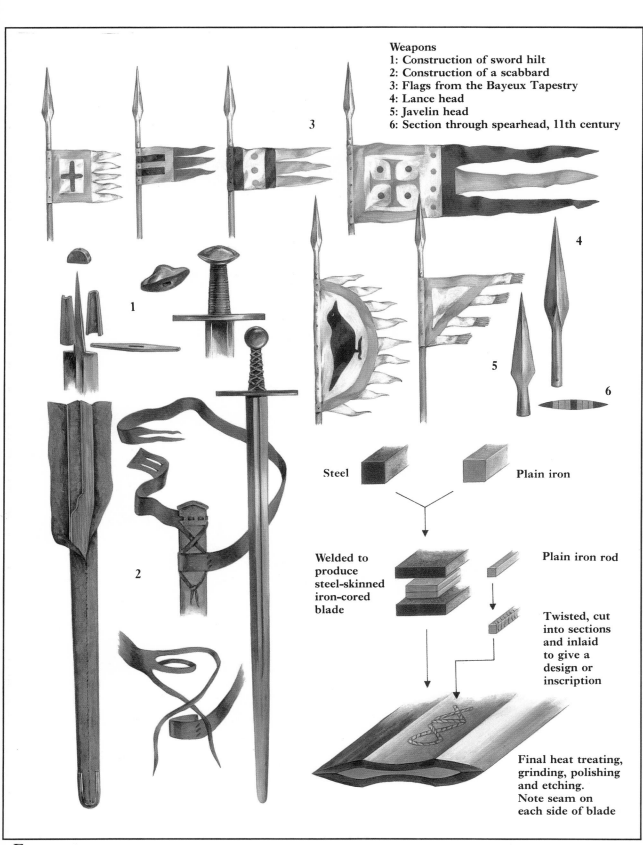

Weapons
1: Construction of sword hilt
2: Construction of a scabbard
3: Flags from the Bayeux Tapestry
4: Lance head
5: Javelin head
6: Section through spearhead, 11th century

3

1

2

4

5

6

Steel

Plain iron

Welded to
produce
steel-skinned
iron-cored
blade

Plain iron rod

Twisted, cut
into sections
and inlaid
to give a
design or
inscription

Final heat treating,
grinding, polishing
and etching.
Note seam on
each side of blade

F

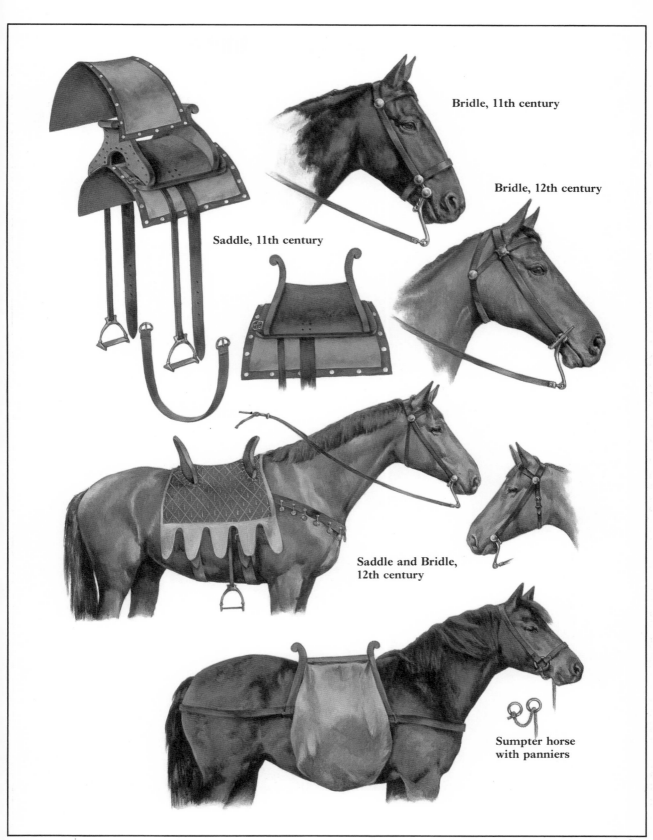

Bridle, 11th century

Bridle, 12th century

Saddle, 11th century

Saddle and Bridle, 12th century

Sumpter horse with panniers

G

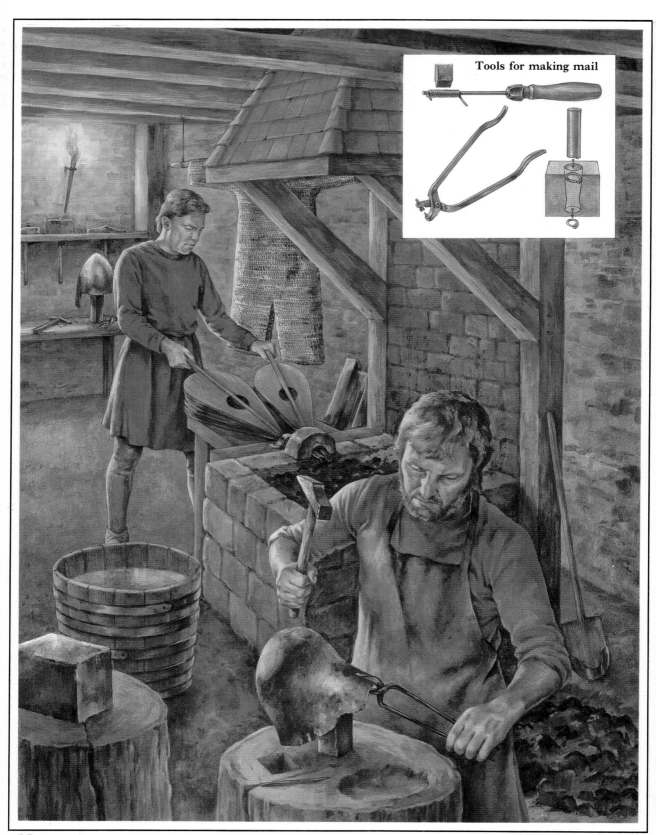

Tools for making mail

The armourer's workshop

I

J

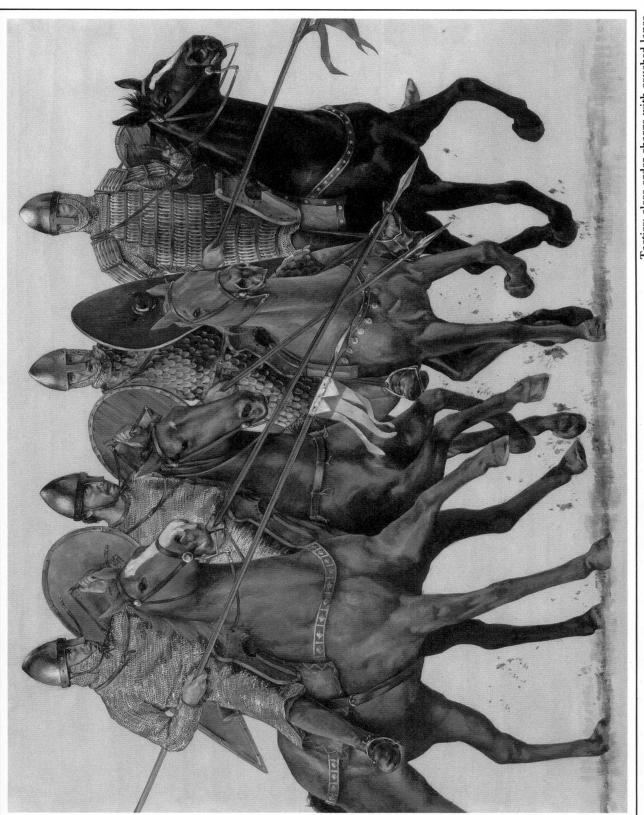

Tactics; close order charge with couched lance

Knight, c.1190: Robert FitzWalter

Mail muffler

Arrangement of
mail hose

Arms of
Robert FitzWalter

L

patrolled, surprised French raiders who were on their way to besiege it. A large-scale ambush was that of Duke William's attack on the French/Angevin rear, trapped by the tide while crossing the ford at Varaville in 1057.

# MOTIVATION

The sons of the Norman nobility, like those in other parts of western Europe, had limited opportunities. The eldest, especially in England, would usually inherit the patrimony but for the rest the main outlet was either the church or a military career. The eldest was expected to become a knight, other younger sons who chose war as a profession also found knighthood expedient. Some became vassals of great lords, receiving land or living as household knights. Some would marry a rich heiress and so obtain land; some would become rich through tournaments. Others became soldiers of fortune, seeking wealth abroad and eventually carving out kingdoms in Italy, Sicily and the Holy Land. Still others hired themselves out as mercenaries. Thus Norman knights sold their services to the Byzantine Emperor soon after arriving in Italy. All were endeavouring to promote their career in a harsh world which, to men of their birth, offered only the church as an alternative.

We know from Orderic that not all such men were uncultured, for the knights of Maule used to enjoy holding academic conversations with the monks in the cloisters of the priory there. Others, such as the Earl of Chester, had a noisy household crowded with men and dogs. He was a man who uncaringly rode roughshod over the crops of his peasant tenants when out hunting yet was careful to keep a poet at his court. In the 11th century knights were brought up on epic tales of heroes, stories short on love interest and long on blood and fighting. In the 12th century courtly love themes crept slowly in from southern France and romances, often with Arthurian themes, began to arise. Moreover there was a certain *esprit de corps* among knights, even if often for the fact that a captured knight meant ransom money. Loyalty to your lord was, however, an important concept, as was honour. Peasants fared badly during unrest and footsoldiers were cut down with impunity after a defeat. A few men were exceptionally cruel and treacherous; Robert of Bellême had a liking for torturing prisoners rather than ransoming them. Yet men were not unaware of the evil they did. The Conqueror on his deathbed was, so it was reported, weighed down by guilt at the blood he had shed. Some knights, after a life of violence, took the cross

*A mailcoat, split at the sides in the old fashion, is worn by this warrior in a depiction of the* Massacre of the Innocents. *His sword is carried under the mail but on the right side rather than the left, possibly a mistake of the artist. (By permission of the British Library, Ms Cotton Nero C 4 f.14)*

and went on a pilgrimage or crusade. Others entered monasteries so they would die in monkish robes, for nearly all believed ultimately in God's power.

It is obvious from the many speeches made by commanders before battle that their soldiers needed enouragement and that they were often nervous of the outcome and feared death. This was used to advantage in the Crusades by the reassurance that those who died would go straight to heaven. Men also feared defeat, which prevented many battles from developing in the first place. Older and wiser minds often tried to persuade younger commanders against making a stand, because of the dangers inherent in losing a pitched battle, often with good reason. It was safer to destroy villages and crops, to show up an enemy's failure as a protective lord, and to threaten war, than to actually engage in it. Some men avoided becoming knights by paying scutage instead. Originally this was a money payment raised on those too young, sick or old to become knights and probably used in England during the reign of Rufus. However, already in Henry I's time the sheer cost of becoming a knight caused some to pay scutage. Finance outweighed ideas of chivalry.

# BOHEMOND

Tall, broad-shouldered, muscular, slim-hipped but slightly stooping, white-skinned with a clean-shaven face where the white mingled with red, blue-grey eyes and blond hair cut to the ears; this portrait of Bohemond of Taranto comes down to us from the Byzantine princess, Anna Comnena, who saw him when a young girl. Despite a certain charm, she recalls how forbidding and savage he seemed, how untrustworthy he was and how quickly he changed his mood to suit the moment.

Bohemond was the son of Robert Guiscard, the tough Norman adventurer who had arrived in Italy in

1041 and carved himself a large slice of southern Italy. Bohemond was born to Aubrée and christened Mark but because of his size in his mother's womb received the nickname of Bohemond after a giant of that name.

The boy soon took after his father and joined him on his aggressive sojourns. In 1080 Guiscard, under a papal banner and probably with an eye on the imperial throne, set sail from Otranto with Bohemond. Having captured Corfu they advanced on Durazzo. Although Guiscard had to return to Italy to help the Pope and quell a revolt, Bohemond was left to press the attack. So adroit was he that he almost reached Constantinople itself before being rebuffed at Larissa in 1083, when the Byzantines themselves are said to have used a feigned flight. The Normans were now steadily pushed back and the Balkans lost.

When Guiscard died in 1085 his son, Roger 'Borsa', was designated his successor. Angry at being

*St Edmund routs the Danes, a manuscript of 1125–1150. Here the lances are shown couched in the prevalent 12th-century fashion, though one rider uses his to stab a fallen warrior. The rider at lower left has horizontal ties across his saddle bows which may be to secure an overblanket. Notice also the figure at lower right who wears a coif and tunic as well as a long underskirt. (Pierpont Morgan Library M.736 f7v.)*

disinherited by his lacklustre half-brother, Bohemond immediately seized Oria, Otranto and Taranto and in 1090 took Bari as well. He was only stopped by the formidable Roger, 'Great Count' and conqueror of Sicily, who now pushed north to consolidate and increase his possessions in southern Italy.

In 1096, contingents of knights who formed part of the 1st Crusade rode into the shifting political struggles of southern Italy. While Borsa and Roger were uninterested, Bohemond took the Crusader's oath and set off. Although he possibly had some genuine desire to free the Holy Places, he may also have seen an opportunity to revive his expansionist designs, either in the Empire or in the east. Having passed through an uneasy Constantinople with his followers, he took a prominent part in the battle of Dorylaeum against the Turks; by the time they reached Antioch late in 1097, Bohemond was an acknowledged leader.

Antioch would be a suitable prize, and Bohemond went all out to acquire it for himself. He defeated relief forces by keeping his own men in reserve until the Muslims thought victory was theirs. A second relief force from Aleppo was also broken

*An ivory altar back shows southern Italian warriors wearing what appears to be scale armour, with helmets similar in style to that seen on the mounted chessman. Is this a form of early attached neck-guard (aventail) or simply a deep helmet over a coif? (Salerno, Cathedral Museum)*

when the crusading cavalry lay in wait. Although the first mounted charge by the Crusaders failed to break the large force, it was then lured on to ground with a lake on the left and river on the right where the Christians were protected against flank attack. A final full charge then broke it. Bohemond led the assault which took the city on 3 June 1098, assisted by treachery within. He also led the whole army out to defeat Kerbogha who had arrived to take back the city, in the most complete victory of the 1st Crusade. In this he emerged from the city with the footsoldiers in a screen to protect the horsemen until the critical moment. The mounted charge which followed crashed into the enemy ranks and secured the ultimate victory. In the face of this his request to take possession of Antioch was unopposed except by Raymond of Toulouse, whose own men finally forced him to leave Bohemond in Antioch. Careful to legitimise his position after the fashion of Norman conquerors in Italy, Bohemond was invested as

Prince of Antioch in 1100 by Daimbert, Archbishop of Pisa and papal legate, thus cutting himself from the Byzantine Emperor and from any interference from Jerusalem.

In 1100 Bohemond was captured by the Turks and only released three years later. Returning to the west he was treated as a super-hero and began stirring enmity against the Emperor Alexis, accusing him of treachery in having turned back from Antioch when the Crusaders needed him. In 1106 Bohemond, newly married to the daughter of the king of France, preached a crusade in Chartres cathedral against Alexis. The following year, with papal backing, this restless warrior moved once again against the Byzantine Empire. Knowing Antioch was safe under his warlike nephew, Tancred, he set about besieging Dyrrhachium, the fortress guarding the gateway to the Balkans. When assault proved useless, Bohemond sat down to starve it into submission. Unfortunately, Byzantine ships thwarted his plans, blockading the coast and cutting him off from Italy. Soon the Byzantine army, with Turkish mercenaries, hemmed him in and waited. Trapped, his own men dropping with disease and famine, the Prince had no option but to surrender to Alexis in September, 1108. Forced to agree a treaty with the Emperor, he returned humiliated to Apulia and died three years later.

# LOGISTICS

An apprentice to arms would be supplied by his lord with the items necessary for his training. He might possess a sword or even some armour as a gift from his father. Alternatively arms, armour and horse might be received from the lord who knighted him or even the lord who took him into his service, an echo of the old Germanic idea of the lord as gift-giver. Less romantically, such possessions might come from battlefield looting, the ransoming of captured knights or as spoils from the tournament. Any weapons or armour received in this way might be given to one's own followers, since their appearance reflected the generosity and wealth of their master. Alternatively such booty could be sold and the money used for other purposes.

Mail, helmet and sword were tough and might take a fair amount of punishment before they needed replacement rather than repair. Mail in particular was long-lasting since any damage could be mended with new rings. This was just as well considering the cost of such equipment. Shields and lances, on the other hand, might need regular replacement depending on the frequency of action. For knights living in a lord's household the cost was borne by the lord; for those on estates the bill was laid at their own door. Warhorses cost a fortune, one reason a knight was set above other men, and the loss of such an animal through wounds or disease was a real setback to any knight with little financial backing.

Landed knights supplied their own food from the produce of their estates, whereas household knights and mercenaries were fed by the lord. On castle rota, landed knights would be fed at the lord's expense. On campaign the whole force expected the king, duke or lord to make provision for supplying their needs. In

*A mail shirt from Verdal, North Tronderlag, Norway, may be of 14th-century date but gives an idea of the style of coat used earlier. The shirt is worn with the rivet heads of the mail facing outwards so as not to cause wear to either the heads or the undergarment. (University Museum of National Antiquities, Oslo)*

some cases this meant carrying supplies on pack animals or in carts; on the 3rd Crusade Richard I took so much that many of the footsoldiers were forced to carry some of the baggage. However, this was never the whole answer. It was vital that a sizeable force was ensured provisions to keep it in the field. This might be done by fortifying castles to allow a supply line to be kept open through hostile territory, often a slow process. Alternatively a force would simply ravage the surrounding areas, which brought in supplies unless stubborn or careless; when one half of a French/Angeuin invasion force scattered to plunder round Morlemer in 1054 it was set upon by the Normans and destroyed. That is why foraging for food was accompanied often by incendiaries who burned villages and destroyed what they could not take, including peasants and their crops. Squires were often grouped into foraging parties, sometimes accompanied by a knightly escort. This was a far less risky way of waging war than by direct confrontation which might end in disaster. Of course, two could play at that game; keeping an armed force in the vicinity of a hostile invader often rendered him

*A sculpted capital showing the Psychomachia, from Nôtre-Dame-du-Port, Clermont-Ferrand. Although French rather than Norman and of mid 12th-century date, the square form of ventail can be seen hanging down over the chest and laced up on the left-hand figure. Such ventails would not necessarily have covered so much of the face.*

impotent, since he dare not throw out foraging parties. Thus thwarted, supplies would dry up and he would be forced to withdraw.

# MUSEUMS

It should be noted that those wishing to study actual Norman arms and equipment are rather poorly served. Even museums which provide fairly extensive displays of items of the period cannot but give a flavour since so many pieces of arms and armour must be studied in the context of comparable pieces rather than as actual 'Norman' items of the 10th to early 13th century. Examples of armour are extremely rare; only four helmets survive of 'Norman' type and only one of these, in the Metropolitan Museum of Art in

New York, appears to be from northern France or England. Even then there is no proof that it dates from the period under discussion.

The other surviving helmets are from eastern Europe. That supposedly of the 10th-century St. Wenceslas is held by Prague Cathedral along with a mailcoat which has never been fully studied but which may be from the 10th or 11th century.

The Hofjagd-und Rüstkammer in Vienna holds the conical helmet forged in one piece. While a major museum of arms and armour, items of this period are rare and not from a Norman context.

The Royal Armouries at the Tower of London displays the segmented conical helmet on loan from Liverpool Museum. Swords, maces, spears and spurs of the time can also be seen. A 14th-century mailcoat gives an idea of the appearance of this form of armour. The Education centre has replicas of a conical helmet, kite-shaped shield and sword which are used as teaching aids.

The British Museum has a large collection of swords, spears, axes, knives, shield bosses and spurs dating from the migration period up to the 11th century, many of which are held in store.

The British Library is useful for studying manuscript representations of warriors, although many will, of necessity, be included in folios kept in store.

The Centre Guillaume le Conquérant in the Rue de Nesmond, Bayeux, houses the Bayeux Tapestry and provides an introductory display, exhibition and film show as well as the actual embroidery itself.

The Musée des Antiquités at Rouen possesses some artefacts from Viking settlements in Normandy.

The north door and west front of the church of San Nicola, Bari, the ceiling of the Cappella Palatina in Palermo and the cloisters of Monreale Cathedral just outside Palermo, are all sources of pictorial representations of Norman knights and their mixed followings.

Manuscript pictures and sculptures are also scattered throughout museums, churches and cathedrals of Europe.

# THE PLATES

### A: Early knight, c.1000

It is not known for certain at what date the Viking settlers of Normandy adapted themselves to become horsemen in emulation of their Frankish neighbours. Since armoured horsemen had been seen in Carolingian armies a century before, the invaders may have assimilated themselves quite quickly. This man's equipment is essentially old fashioned. He wears a *spangenhelm*, an early style of helmet still used in the 11th century and may even have survived into the 13th century. The initial shape was created by constructing an iron framework consisting of (usually four) vertical strips springing from a browband. The spaces between were then filled with plates, most probably of iron though horn may rarely have been used. A cap secured the apex. Additional lining rivets are provided along the browband. In some cases the nasal may have been formed by extending the front vertical strip downwards. The exact construction at this date remains uncertain as no examples have survived. However, they may be seen occasionally in artistic representations. His mailcoat is split at the sides, a fashion far more suited to use on foot but which appeared infrequently throughout the 11th century and into the 12th. His shield is of traditional circular form and not of the kite-shaped variety only now beginning to appear. Since few shield bosses survive from the 10th century or later, and the fragments of wood attached to their rivets are lacking, it is difficult to reconstruct circular shields. Laminated forms, comprising two layers of wood with the grain of each running at right-angles to increase strength, may have been used. Alternatively, shields, built up from planks probably butted and glued, may have been used. The surface was probably often covered by leather. We know that Anglo-Saxon shields were specified in the 10th century as being covered in bull hide rather than that of sheep. Some shields may not have been covered, especially if made from one piece of wood. Certainly leather, if glued over the surface, would strengthen the planking.

The borders seen on most shields are also unexplained. The most logical solution is that they represent applied borders rather than painted de-signs, since so many show dots or circles as though to represent nail or rivet heads, unless this is simply artistic tradition. Unfortunately, even on earlier circular shields, these strips are extremely rare. Another possibility in some cases is that the holes are for stitching the leather to the shield face. Whether rims were made of iron, bronze, leather or all three can again only be surmised. The curved bands are often depicted in Carolingian, Ottonian, Anglo-Saxon, Viking and even Pictish art over the centuries; they may represent pieces of leather stitched tog-ether, or reinforcing bands of iron.

His sword has been handed down. It is pattern-welded and fitted with a contemporary 'tea-cosy' pommel. The scabbard, of wood covered in leather, has a supporting strap joined to the rear of the belt to hang the weapon at a convenient angle and prevent

*The fallen warrior, in this scene of David and Goliath, wears chausses which show how they were laced under the shoe. Notice the rendition of the chausses, a feature of this period which has led some to argue that different types of armour are being worn. (By permission of the British Library, Add. Ms. 14789 f.10)*

the knight from tripping over it. He may carry javelins as well as a more conventional spear with a sturdy blade. His iron prick spurs are of the cylindrical type used by knights in north-western Europe. The Vikings at this date may have sported hair with a heavy fringe but cut clear of the neck. This knight copies neighbouring warriors in having his hair cut round in a bowl crop, a style which may have been useful when a mail coif was attached to the mailcoat.

## B: Armour

Mail consisted of many individually linked iron rings. Every ring passed through four others, and garments could be shaped by varying the number. Where armpits were formed which would bunch the mail into a knot, a ring might not be joined to all four partners, this being known today as an 'idle' ring. 'Idle' rings were also used to shape other areas.

Scale armour, of iron, bronze, horn, bone or leather plates, was formed by riveting the upper end of each scale through a canvas backing, presumably with a washer on the rear to prevent the rivet working out. Overlapping each scale downwards guarded the rivets of those below. Most illustrations suggest the

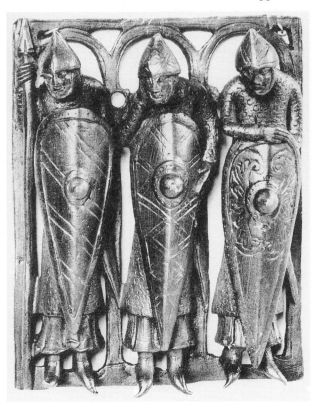

rows were staggered like fish scales, though some suggest vertical lines.

Lamellar, probably only used in Italy and the east, was made by lacing small iron plates together in rows, the whole coat being held by interlacing. These coats were probably tied by laces at the side.

The enigmatical 'square' on the chest of some warriors on the Bayeux Tapestry has caused much debate but no firm conclusion has been reached. Perhaps the most popular theory is that it represents the lowered ventail or flap to guard the throat and chin, which is lifted and tied at the sides of the coif when the knight goes into action. This also enables a neck opening to be made large enough to pull the shirt on and off easily. In support of this theory it may be pointed out that several figures on the Tapestry appear to have the sides pulled up. Moreover, in the scene before action at Hastings, a whole string of horsemen show squares on the chest, whilst those going into action only sport a single bar, presumably the lower edge when lifted. It should also be noted that several Englishmen also have this bar but since it appears near the neck, it may be some sort of edging in the same fashion as those shown at the sleeves and hem. Hauberks carried to the ships are depicted with squares although they show no coifs but here it may be argued that they are hanging down at the back.

Less easy to explain is an Anglo-Saxon depiction of a square on a ringed coat worn by a tiny initial figure, where he appears to have no coif. This problem is also encountered in a few other depictions, mostly on contemporary Spanish figures. Details of a definite ventail flap have to wait until the 12th-century carved figures at Clermont Ferrand in central France. Another suggestion is that the flap guards a slit at the neck to enable the hauberk to be put on. Last, and probably least persuasive, it may be a reinforcing piece of mail over the chest, or even show the supporting straps of a plate of iron beneath the hauberk. There is also the possibility that two or even all three of these versions may have been in use.

*The so-called 'Temple Pyx' of c.1140–50 probably formed part of a reliquary. Made from gilt copper-alloy, the three figures carry typical long shields with simple decoration. The lattice of the central shield is dotted, suggesting riveted reinforcing strips. Two of the helmets also have diagonal bands. (Glasgow Museums and Art Galleries, Burrell Collection)*

INCIPIT LIBER IOSVE BENN VN:

VT. POST. MORE. MOYSI.

*An initial from the Winchester Bible of c.1170 shows knights in flowing surcoats with simple decoration. Their mailcoats have the sleeves extended to cover their hands while leaving the fingers exposed. (Reproduction by permission of the Dean and Chapter of Winchester Cathedral)*

Another style of ventail is the long tongue of mail which is drawn up across the face before combat and laced to a thong at the side of the head. This was certainly in use by the early 12th century. Ventails, which are mentioned in the *Song of Roland* of *c.*1100, may have been lined for added comfort. Some may simply have consisted of a loose vertical slit which was drawn tight by a thong when action was expected. One form of leg protection consisted of a strip of mail, laced behind the leg and braced to the waist girdle.

The Norman shaven head as seen in the Bayeux Tapestry is probably an extreme form of the earlier warrior's bowl crop. It is partly borne out by the remark of Wace, who says that in 1066 Englishmen spying on the Norman camp reported that William had brought an army of priests. The style disappeared in the reign of the Conqueror's son, William Rufus, when long hair and beards were in vogue.

### C: Norman knight, c.1066

The mail hauberk is split front and rear to facilitate movement, particularly when mounted, when the side of the skirt would hang round the thigh. His mail is provided with a coif and ventail. The segmented helmet was perhaps the most common form in use in 1066, to judge from the Bayeux Tapestry. It was constructed from four shaped iron segments riveted together. The browband with nasal was then applied. Contemporary illustrations suggest that this was the most frequently seen method of securing the nasal. The rivet holes could also be used to fix a lining band. This helmet sports a rough and ready repair, the work of a local smith rather than a professional armourer. The shield is now kite-shaped, defending the left side but capable of protecting much of the horse when held out horizontally. This is the attitude usually seen on the Tapestry and may have been common when used by mounted men against footsoldiers. When used against enemy horsemen with couched lances it would be prudent to hold it more vertically to give maximum protection to the left front of the body.

The sword is carried under the mail, a slit at the hip providing access to the scabbard mouth. The earlier occasional use of baldrics seems to have disappeared by the mid 11th century, and the weapon was usually buckled on by a waist belt. His tinned spurs now have a pyramidal spike to goad his horse.

### D: Helmets

A hypothetical view of the inside of a Norman helmet. It must be stressed that very few helmets of the period survive, only one may by northern French, and no linings survive at all. This reconstruction is based on the rivet arrangements of actual helmets combined with the type of linings surviving in later medieval helmets. The leather lining band is secured around the inside of the helmet rim by rivets and crude square washers. To this band the lining itself is stitched. This consists of two layers of canvas stuffed with wool, tow, hay, hair or grass and seamed to keep the stuffing in place. The top edge is also seamed to take a running thong which may be adjusted to ensure the helmet is a firm fit and is aligned with the eyes. This is especially important in later helmets where the face is guarded by a mask with eye slits. In order to make sure the helmet remains on the head, a bifurcated leather chin strap is riveted in place, the two-point fastening making the helmet less likely to wobble. This was probably tied rather than buckled under the chin. On this particular helmet, made from one piece of metal, the slight medial ridge running from front to rear can be seen, beaten out from the inside.

A *spangenhelm* is here shown provided with an applied neck-guard as suggested by the Bayeux Tapestry. The exact width of these guards is not known.

A helmet of the early 12th century has been fashioned from one piece and the surface fluted by beating from the outside. The rear edge has been drawn down to provide a neck-guard, giving the helmet a sou'wester shape. Helmets forged from one piece of iron became increasingly common in the 12th century.

The slight forward peak seen on the previous helmet and typical of the 12th century is seen again on this later 12th-century helmet complete with face-guard, based on a depiction of the murder of Becket painted on a church wall in Spoleto, Italy. The full face mask may have developed from 'T'-bars added to the nasal to protect the mouth. Hemispherical and cylindrical helmets were also occasionally adapted in this way.

The dawning of the 13th century saw the full face-guard joined to the neck-guard to produce the forerunner of the completely enclosing helm which was developed by the 1230s. Cylindrical helmets had become popular towards the end of the 12th century and seem to have been the most common type to be extended into this new design.

### E: Shields

The kite-shaped shield was made of wood. None has survived, so any reconstruction is based on earlier circular shields and later surviving examples. A drawing of a now vanished 12th-century shield from Norway suggests that it was made from planks (presumably) glued side by side. However, surviving 13th-century shields, including one which may have originally been made in the late 12th century, are constructed from a single piece of wood. The leather covering is again hypothetical. It is also just possible that in the 11th century some kite shields were even of laminated construction. Though those seen on the Tapestry appear flat (since dinner is eaten off them) others may have been slightly curved to the wearer (as Anna Comnena noted of those carried by Italian Normans).

The borders of kite shields may have been painted but numerous depictions with dots or circles suggest that, like circular shields, they had some form of edging. On 13th-century shields depictions of such edges again become rare, often remaining only as a heraldic border.

Shield straps (brases or enarmes) appear to have a variety of shapes. Many on the Bayeux Tapestry are shown as a simple strap across the top edge, but some strap for the forearm was presumably necessary also. Other depictions are more complex, several showing a pair of crossed straps for the hand, a common method represented elsewhere and continued into the 12th century and beyond. The rectangle of straps, occasionally in the form of a diamond, is more confined to the Bayeux Tapestry. It may be assumed that a stuffed pad was nailed on to protect at least the fist and possibly the forearm, as seen on surviving 13th-century shields. The guige strap was probably provided with a buckle to adjust the length, though these are rarely seen in art. Some brases may also have been adjustable.

The iron, bronze or brass boss was a throwback to the circular shield but as it was no longer in a central position the shield was held by straps, relegating the boss to a decorative role. As a fashion it lasted into the 13th century. The rivet heads would be seen on the inside of the shield unless covered by the pad. Some shields might have been entirely covered on the inside by parchment or even leather. The rivet heads of the straps would be seen on the outer face. The boss might be used to form a decorative design with

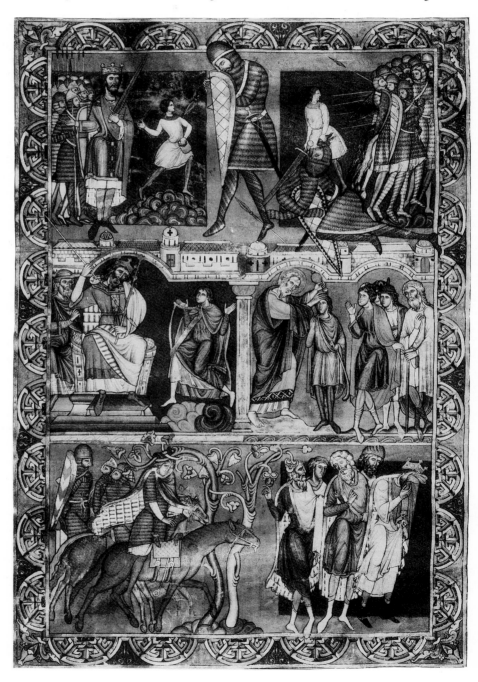

*'David and Goliath' and 'The Death of Absolom' from the Winchester Bible depicts mailed men whose hands are completely covered to form mufflers. The horse at lower left has a cloth laid over the saddle, provided with slits to pass over the arçons. (Pierpont Morgan Library, M. 619 v.)*

these, or they might be incorporated into a zoomorphic shape.

Twelfth-century shields often had a flattened top but frequently retained rounded corners. Many were curved to the wearer. The strap arrangements differed little from the previous century and are often simplified in art. Straps, probably of metal, are sometimes seen on shield faces, radiating from the boss in a decorative design which also strengthened the shield. Such designs also passed into heraldic usage.

## F: Weapons

The sword was the most prized of weapons. Pattern-welded forms were made from bundles of twisted rods of iron and mild steel (carburised iron), forged together, beaten and twisted until the blade was formed. It retained the wavy design along its surface, hence the name. Pattern-welded swords were made in a variety of combinations of iron and mild steel. Swords made from iron and steel were also forged in a variety of ways, some of which are illustrated here. Many swordsmiths probably took their secrets to the grave.

The hilt of a sword was formed by first sliding the cross-guard down until it rested against the shoulders of the blade. The grip was formed from two halves of carved wood which were presumably glued together around the tang. The pommel—here of tea-cosy form—was slotted over the end and the tip of the tang hammered over to hold the components in place. The grip could be left as plain wood, but it would usually be bound additionally. This might have taken the form of a soft leather sheath stitched at the side and shrunk on to the grip, or else a strip bound up it. Some swords would probably be further embellished by an interlaced cord which not only gave an attractive appearance but helped to form a rough grip for a sweating hand. The earliest surviving grips are of 13th-century date but 12th-century illustrations suggest similar forms were used earlier. A lobated pommel, a late survivor of an earlier style, is also shown.

Most swords had straight or slightly curved cross-guards which helped prevent a weapon from sliding up the blade to the hand. Some knights may have hooked their forefinger over the guard to assist in controlling their weapon. Many hilts are quite small, suggesting that the sword was sometimes held with the pommel actually within the lower part of the palm. This is a simple wheel pommel.

Scabbards were made from two slats of wood

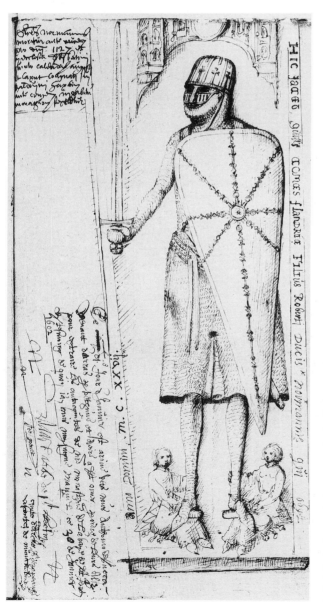

*A sketch made of the now lost 12th-century effigy of William Clito (died 1127), Count of Flanders and son of Duke Robert of Normandy. His face is protected by a steel mask formed by expanding the nasal and which appears to be pierced with vertical slots for ventilation. The decorative crosses on the helmet may be a mark of rank, a sort of modified coronet. A ventail is drawn diagonally across the face and secured at the left temple. The shield bands are both decorative and act as reinforcement.*

covered with leather and lined with wool, fur or parchment. Tenth- and 11th-century chapes might be of openwork design but by the 12th century a simple 'U' shape seems more usual. The scarcity of survivors suggests that many swords were simply bound at the tip with an extra layer of leather or had no chape at all. Lockets, too, might be of openwork design or even of bone but few have come down to us from the 11th or 12th century, possibly because the means of fastening the sword was altering. The method of attaching the sword belt to the scabbard in the 10th and 11th century is not known for certain. In some cases additional suspension straps may have been used. The Bayeux Tapestry almost seems to suggest a stud fastening similar to early Germanic varieties. Other illustrations, especially in the 12th century, frequently depict a cross of straps which strongly suggests the type of fixing used in the 13th century. In this, the shorter end of the belt was split, one piece being threaded through slits cut in the

scabbard leather while two others passed down and were laced together. By threading through slits cut in the other part of the belt, the two halves were prevented from sliding apart while keeping the sword at a convenient angle. Sometimes only one strip passed down between the upper and lower belt halves.

The lance, probably of ash wood, was fitted with an iron head provided with a socket in which the shaft was secured by a nail. The flags have been drawn from the Bayeux Tapestry, including what is probably the papal banner blessed for the invasion of England. The semicircular flag seems likely to be a representation of the raven banner used by the pagan Danes. Knights of rank were marked by a small pennon nailed below their lance head.

### G: Horses

The saddles shown on the Bayeux Tapestry and a number of other representations do not give a great

*The second great seal of Richard I, struck in 1194 on his release from captivity. Despite popular opinion, the King is not shown wearing a surcoat. A long undergarment issues from beneath his mail. The shield now carries the three lions of England for the first time. His helm is quite advanced, almost fully covering the head and provided with a fan crest, presumably of metal, on which are echoed the lions of the shield. (Public Records Office, London)*

amount of detail. The pommel and cantle on most appear to curl outwards at the upper end and the saddles are usually reconstructed with a scrolled top edge. The very few depictions of contemporary saddles to show the face of the saddle arçons come from southern France and Italy. While the French example also shows a curved profile, the cantle shown end on has a rounded edge, echoed in the front view from the Italian illustration. Were these examples also used in the north or are they more typical of the south? We have reconstructed both versions. The saddles are basic: a tree of two pieces set either side of the horse's spine, the arçons carved to shape and with a central cut-out at the lower edge. Some form of padding would be nailed over the gap between the trees and a leather seat attached.

The stirrups are long. The leathers pass under the saddle flap, probably looping through a slot cut in the tree and buckling under the saddle flap. Less likely, a metal loop might be nailed to the tree through which the leathers are looped. The girths are nailed to the saddle and buckle on both sides to allow for adjustment. Breast straps and any crupper straps would probably be attached either through a ring nailed to the tree or, if it did not project far enough, to the saddle bow itself. Such straps might occassionally be decorated with metal plaques or pendants, especially in the 12th century. A saddle blanket is worn

below the saddle to stop chafing. An overblanket may have been placed over the saddle for comfort and may provide another interpretation of the shape of saddles on the Bayeux Tapestry, though other sources definitely do not show these. At least two manuscripts of the early 12th century appear to show cords passing over the sides of the saddle bows and disappearing under the rider. These may be for securing such an overblanket.

The bridle is of simple form and provided with a curb bit, most of these having their arms apparently joined by a transverse bar. The curb chain is positioned under the jaw. Illustrations rarely show any buckles on the cheek pieces, even on later and more detailed representations. The reins, some of which appear to have ended in metal decorative tabs, were knotted together and most probably had a running ring for adjustment, a feature very occasionally seen in representations. Throughout the period the brow-band is replaced occasionally by slits cut in the leather through which the ears pass.

Twelfth-century saddles at first appear similar to the foregoing but as the century progresses the cantle develops a slightly more upright form and becomes more curved to the rider, while the front of the saddle bow often curved away from him. This form is less like a pommel but more like the wider form seen in the southern European illustrations. Some arçons may have been painted. Crupper straps appear in art more frequently. Sometimes, as here, large decorative overblankets (often with dagged lower edges) are worn, the arçons passing through slits cut in the fabric.

Twelfth-century bridles often have no nose-band but some have a neck strap which sometimes joins to an extension of the brow-band.

A sumpter horse is shown with a saddle fitted with panniers. A leading rope is passed through the ring of the headstall. Others would be entirely of simple rope construction.

*David and Goliath, from the Great Canterbury Psalter of about 1180–90. The edging of the mailcoat is seen on a number of illustrations but has never been satisfactorily explained. It may be a simple leather binding to stop the rings rubbing the undergarment, or even the edge of an attached lining. It seems unlikely to be a loose padded aketon since here the dog-leg edge follows the mail exactly while the undergarment is clearly shown as separate. (Bibliothèque Nationale, Ms. Lat. 8846, f.2v)*

*Iron sword chapes of the later 12th or 13th century. These are plain, functional items lacking the embellishments or openwork piercing of 10th- or even some 11th-century examples. (By kind permission of Anthony de Reuck)*

## H: The armourer's workshop

Workshops are likely to have been of detached stone construction because of the dangers of fire. Some may even have been used to smelt the iron. This forge has a stone-built hearth with a canopy of earthenware tiles to draw the smoke away. A pair of hand-pumped bellows supplies the draught through metal tuyères over which a traditional semicircular and stone is placed. In front, set into a tree trunk, is a rectangular iron anvil. This is the shape usually associated with armourers, although occasionally the more familiar pointed variety is shown in artistic representations. Charcoal helps to keep the fire hot. Windows would be kept to a minimum or omitted entirely. A torch gives light and this controllable source means the armourer can see when the metal in the fire has reached the right temperature by the colour it becomes or the sparks that adhere to its surface.

The other tree trunk has holes to take iron formers or stakes shaped like mushrooms. Here a conical helmet has been heated and is being beaten out. The slight depression in the top surface of the trunk is for shaping shallow pieces of metal, such as helmet segments, from the inside. The tub of water is for quenching hot metal after shaping. Tools include tongs for holding hot metal, various sizes of hammers, some for planishing or shaping cold metal, a wooden mallet for less violent beating, files and awls. Suggested tools for making mail are also shown.

## I: The hunt

Hunting was a tough sport and knights were killed in accidents. Sometimes the quarry was directed past the greyhounds who then gave chase. In this scene from the early 12th century a boar has been brought to bay by greyhounds and is grappled by heavier alaunts, powerful dogs which were often hard to handle. The knight, distinguished from the squires by his long hair, has elected to attack from horseback, which needs skill in controlling his mount and a steady aim. The boar spear has lugs to stop an enraged boar from running too far on to it. Should the boar break free another huntsman may demonstrate his courage by trying to stab it while on foot. The use of the bow and crossbow in the hunting field was probably the only time a knight or squire would carry one.

The hunting party essentially wear civilian attire similar to that worn under their armour. Despite this the knight still carries his sword and rides a stallion.

## J: Gerberoi

Shortly after Christmas, 1078, King William I marched on the castle of Gerberoi, near Beauvais and the eastern borders of Normandy, to besiege his rebellious son, Robert. Three weeks later Robert sallied out and attacked the besiegers. During the fighting William, now corpulent and about 50 years

*This portrayal of the murder of Thomas Becket dates to the late 12th or early 13th century and illustrates a form of helmet which seems to be provided with a solid chin-guard, a feature rarely seen elsewhere. The bear on the shield alludes to Reginald FitzUrse, one of the murderers. (By permission of the British Library, Ms. Harley 5102 f.32)*

old, had his horse killed beneath him, possibly by Robert himself. Wounded in the arm, the King was saved ironically by an Englishman in his army named Toki, who sprang down and gave William his own horse. Toki was then himself killed by a crossbow bolt. The King's other son, William Rufus, fighting on his father's side, was also wounded and Robert retired with his troops.

Such a downfall was the greatest humiliation in the King's career, said the 12th-century chronicler, William of Malmesbury. Being unhorsed was bad enough. That in itself could cause severe panic, as had the rumour of William's death at Hastings. Here, however, he had also lost the fight, especially unsettling when his troops were fighting other Nor-

mans. In many such contests in Normandy and the neighbouring areas after the Conquest, Normans in the royal army faced those led by a rebellious son or brother. In such cases both sides might use similar tactics and the outcome, unlike many conflicts in Italy, was less clear.

### K: The couched lance

Normans in Italy charge Byzantines, who hated the solid lines of horsemen with levelled lances. This solid tactic was now becoming the usual method for a cohesive charge, as the 11th century ended and the 12th began. Though many knights wore the same armour as seen in the west, some were influenced by more eastern styles encountered in Byzantine Italy and Sicily with its overlays of Muslim culture. Some wear scale armour, seen also in the west, while others are dressed in coats of lamella probably tied at the left side so that the shield protected the laces. The audacious Normans with their fighting ability and lust for land used their prowess to profitable ends. Led by hard-bitten men such as Robert Guiscard and Bohemond, they succeeded in breaking enemy forces in a number of engagements in Italy and Sicily and subsequently took their fighting methods to the Crusades, modifying them to suit the tactics encountered there.

### L: Knight, c.1190

This knight is dressed in the latest equipment. Although some knights still looked similar to those at Hastings, changes had occurred. The lower edge of the mail skirt has shortened to rest above the knee and the sleeves are elongated into mail mufflers with a cloth palm. A lace threaded through the links helps to keep the mail in place. Mail hose enclose the leg and are braced up to the waist girdle on the braies in a similar way to the cloth hose worn beneath and into which the braies are tucked. A lace below the knee helps to stop the mail from sagging at this point. A surcoat is now worn over the mail and belted at the waist. The helmet is cylindrical and flat-topped and is fitted with a rigid face-guard pierced for ventilation. The spurs are still of the prick variety but the arms now have a curve to accommodate the ankle bone. The shield is a little smaller and flat-topped, the heraldic arms on the front showing this to be Robert FitzWalter, one of the barons who forced King John

to agree to Magna Carta. The arms are not repeated on the surcoat, this being uncommon. The sword is of the latest type, with a slight taper and shorter fuller. It is fitted with a circular disc pommel, the commonest form of the next century. The two halves of the sword belt, like the majority in the 12th and 13th century, are joined by knotting bifurcated ends through two slits. The strap arrangement on the scabbard holds it at a convenient angle.

*A shield of the von Brienze family. This example was probably made in the late 12th century, being modified between 1230 and 1250 by having the top arch cut off. The wood, 15 mm thick, is covered on both sides with parchment and the lion is painted silver on a blue field. The rear straps have been cut away, leaving fragments held by rectangular washers; there are traces of the pad for the fist. Originally the shield may have been about 100 cm long. (Swiss National Museum, Zürich, LM 3405. 178)*

### Further reading

Bennett, Matthew, *La Règle du Temple as a Military Manual or How to Deliver a Cavalry Charge*, Studies in Medieval History Presented to R. Allen Brown, 1989 pp.7–19.

Bennett, Matthew, *The Status of the Squire, the Northern Evidence*, The ideals and Practice of Medieval Knighthood, 1986.

Bennett, Matthew, *Wace and Warfare*, Anglo-Norman Studies XI, 1989, pp.37–57.

Bradbury, Jim, *Battles in England and Normandy*, Anglo-Norman Studies VI, 1984, pp.1–12.

Brown, R.A., *The Normans and the Norman Conquest*, London, 1969. Good standard text.

Brown, R.A., *The Status of the Norman Knight*, War and Government in the Middle Ages, ed. Holt and Gillingham, 1984, pp.18–32.

Chibnall, Marjorie, *Feudal Society in Orderic Vitalis*, Proceedings of the Battle Abbey Conference 1978, 1979, pp.35–48.

Davis, R.H.C., *The Warhorses of the Normans*, Anglo-Norman Studies X, 1988, pp.67–82.

Douglas, D., *William the Conqueror*, London, 1964. A classic reference work.

Douglas, D., *The Norman Achievement*, London, 1969. Includes Italy and Sicily.

Gillingham, John, *Richard I and the Science of War in the Middle Ages*, War and Government in the Middle Ages, ed. Holt and Gillingham, 1984, pp.78–91.

Gravett, Christopher, *Hastings, 1066*, London. 1992. Includes arms, armour and costume.

Heath, Ian, *Armies of the Dark Ages*, Wargames Research Group, 1977.

Heath, Ian, *Armies of Feudal Europe*, Wargames Research Group, 1978.

Hill, Rosalind, *Crusading Warfare: A Camp-follower's View 1097–1120*, Proceedings of the Battle Abbey Conference 1978, 1979, pp.75–83.

Nicolle, David, *The Normans*, London, 1987. An Osprey volume with colour reconstructions.

Norman, Vesey, *The Medieval Soldier*, London, 1971. Detailed coverage of arms, armour and tactics of the period.

Paterson, Linda M., *Military Surgery: Knights, Sergeants, and Raimon of Avignon's Version of the Chirurgia of Roger of Salerno (1180–1209)*, The Ideals and Practice of Medieval Knighthood II, 1988, pp.117–146.

Stenton, F., *The Bayeux Tapestry*, London, second edn. 1965. Includes a good basic description of arms and armour written by the late Sir James Mann, Master of the Armouries at the Royal Armouries. Also a section on costume.

Wilson, D., *The Bayeux Tapestry*, London, 1985. Excellent colour reproduction plus text, including coverage of arms and armour.

The silver seal die of Robert FitzWalter, probably dating to the early 13th century. The enclosing helm is rather similar to that of Richard I. The knight wears a surcoat and his horse a long caparison or trapper which bears his arms. The testier or head covering may be of pourpoint to guard the animal's head. *(Reproduced by courtesy of the Trustees of the British Museum)*

# GLOSSARY

**Aketon** A padded garment, quilted to keep the stuffing in place, worn under or instead of armour. First mentioned in the 12th century.

**Arçon** The saddle bow and cantle.

**Bailey** Courtyard of a castle.

**Baldric** Belt slung across the right shoulder, occasionally used to suspend the sword in the 10th and early 11th century.

**Boss** Metal hand-guard on circular shield; decorative on kite-shaped shields.

**Braies** Linen drawers.

**Brases** Straps for holding a shield.

**Cantle** The rear projection of a saddle.

**Caparison** Cloth covering for a horse, introduced in the later 12th century.

**Chape** Guard fitted to end of scabbard.

**Chausses** Leggings of cloth or mail.

**Coif** Headwear of cloth, usually quilted for military use; a mail hood.

**Conroi** Squadron of horsemen, usually 25 or 50 in number.

**Curb** Bit with long levers to which the rein is attached.

**Destrier** The warhorse.

**Donjon** The great tower of a castle, usually of stone.

**Enarmes** See 'Brases'.

**Fuller** Groove running down a sword blade to lighten it.

**Gambeson** See 'Aketon'.

**Gonfalon, Gonfanon** Penon carried by a baron.

**Guige** Strap supporting shield round the neck, or for hanging it up when not in use.

**Hauberk** Originally a neck-guard. Usually used to refer to the body armour.

**Helm** Helmet enclosing the whole head.

**Hilt** The cross-guard, grip and pommel of a sword.

**Housing** See 'Caparison'.

**Infulae** Pair of cloth strips worn on the rear of the helmet by men of rank.

**Keep** See 'Donjon'.

**Kettle Hat** Open helmet so-called from its likeness to an upturned cauldron.

**Lamellar** Armour composed of small metal strips laced together. Uncommon in north-western Europe.

A 12th- or 13th-century mace head made from copper-alloy. Although light in comparison to later maces, such a weapon could inflict damage to unarmoured opponents or even through flexible mail. (Reproduced by courtesy of the Trustees of the British Museum)

**Locket** Metal, ivory or bone guard for the mouth of the scabbard.

**Mail** Armour composed of many interlinked iron rings.

**Motte** Artificial earthen mound carrying a tower, usually of timber.

**Muffler** Mail mitten formed by extending the sleeve.

**Nasal** Nose-guard.

**Palfrey** A good riding horse.

**Pattern-welded** Method of making a sword blade by twisted rods of iron and carburised iron. Less common after *c*.900 but continued for making spear-heads and knives.

**Pommel** The weighted end of a hilt, to counter-balance the blade; the knob on a saddle bow.

**Pourpoint** See 'Aketon'.

**Prick Spur** One with a pointed terminal.

**Ring-work** Castle consisting of a bailey only.

**Rouncy** An ordinary riding horse.

**Scale** Armour composed of overlapping metal, bone, horn or leather scales.

**Scutage** The commuting of knight service by a money payment introduced in the 12th century.
**Snaffle** Ring bit.
**Sumpter** A pack horse.
**Surcoat** Cloth garment worn over armour.

**Testier** Padded head defence for a horse.
**Trapper** See 'Caparison'.
**Tree** The wooden framework of a saddle.
**Ventail** Flap of mail laced up to protect the throat and lower part of the face.

---

## Notes sur les planches en couleur

**A** Chevalier portant un casque à paillettes (fabriqué en construisant une carcasse avec des plaques de fer et une casquette attachant le tout au sommet) avec une cotte de mailles à fente. Le bouclier est un modèle circulaire traditionnel. L'épée soudée, porte un motif et le pommeau est contemporain. Le fourreau, fait de bois couvert de cuir, est attaché à un angle pour empêcher le chevalier de trébucher. On voit souvent les éperons pointus cylindriques dans le nord-ouest de l'Europe.

**B** Les mailles sont fabriquées avec des anneaux liés, et chaque anneau passe à traverse quatre autres. Les habits sont faits en augmentant ou en réduisant le nombre d'anneaux. L'armure à écaille est fabriquée en rivetant les écailles à travers un support. L'armure à lamelles est faite en lacant des plaques en rangées qui sont ensuite entrelacés.

**C** L'armure de mailles est fendue à l'avant et à l'arrière pour faciliter le mouvement et la maille a une coiffe et un ventail. On voit le plus souvent le casque à segments sur la Tapisserie de Bayeux. Le bouclier est en forme de cerf-volant tandis que l'épée est portée sous la cotte de mailles qui est fendue pour en faciliter l'accès.

**D** Peu de casques survivent et on ne retrouve pas de doublures, mais cependant cette reconstruction illustre la bande de doublure en cuir, rivée à la bordure. La lanière double au menton maintient le casque en position. Les casques qui sont forgés à partir d'une seule pièce de métal sont de plus en plus communs au 12ème siècle, tandis que la visière commence à se developper à la fin du 12ème siècle. Au 13ème siècle on voit la protection intégrale rejoindre le cou, préfigurant le casque complètement fermé développé dans les années 1230.

**E** La reconstruction du bouclier cerf-volant est une hypothèse car on n'en retrouve aucun exemple. Fabriqué avec des planches en bois, on y trouvait peut-être un couvercle peint en cuir et une bordure de quelque sorte. L'ombon en fer, bronze ou cuivre à peut-être pour origine le bouclier circulaire décoratif. Les boucliers du 12ème siècle ont souvent le haut aplati et sont incurvés vers celui qui les porte.

**F** Les épées soudées à motif sont fabriquées à partir de tas de tiges de fer et d'acier tordues, qui sont ensuite forgés et martelés ensemble jusqu'à ce que la lame se forme. On fait la poignée en glissant la garde de l'épée jusqu'à la partie haute de la lame et en collant au dessus deux morceaux de bois l'un à l'autre. Le pommeau s'emboîte par dessus. Le poignée est d'habitude reliée avec du cuir doux. Les lancettes sont probablement fabriquées en bois de saule avec une tête de fer et un trou pour la hampe. Les drapeaux sont ceux de la Tapisserie de Bayeux.

**G** Les selles sont très simples. Une construction en bois à deux pièces – un morceau de chaque côté de l'épine dorsale du cheval, l'arçon, ciselés et un morceau central est enlevé de la bordure du bas. On cloue le rembourrage par dessus le vide entre les deux morceaux et on y attache un siège en cuir. On utilise une couverture sur la selle pour éviter le frottement. La bride est simple avec le mors placé sous la mâchoire. Les reines sont nouées ensemble. Les selles du 12ème siècle sont semblables mais l'arrière devient plus vertical, et les brides n'ont pas, souvent de lanière sur le nez. Le cheval 'sumpter' porte une selle avec des paniers.

**H** Les ateliers sont probablement construits en pierre pour éviter le feu. Le foyer est en pierre, surmonté de tuiles de terre cuite pour la fumée. Le soufflet manuel fournit le courant d'air pour le feu. Une torche fournit une source de lumière controlable permettant à l'armurier de juger l'état du metal qui chauffe par sa couleur. On trouve deux troncs d'arbre, l'un avec une enclume et l'autre avec des trous où on installe les pieus pour marteller les casques.

**I** Le sanglier a été rabattu par les lévriers et se bat avec 'l'alaunt'. Le chavalier se distingue des écuyers par ses cheveux plus longs. La lance pour le sanglier a des tenons pour l'empêcher de pénétrer trop loin. La chasse est le seul moment où le chevalier ou l'écuyer portent un arc. Les autres portent en général l'habit civil.

**J** En 1078 Guillaume ler a marché sur Gerberoi pour assaillir Robert, son fils rebelle. Robert l'attaque. Le cheval de Guillaume meurt, lui-même est blessé. Il est sauvé par un anglais appelé Toki qui lui donne son cheval mais qui est tué plus tard par un carreau d'arbalète. Perdre la bataille et avoir son cheval tué sous lui, c'est la plus grande humiliation de la carrière du Roi.

**K** En Italie, les Normands ont eu de grands succès contre les Byzantins en chargant avec lignes denses de cavaliers armés de lances à leurs côtés. Tandis que plusieurs chevaliers portent l'armure en vigueur en occident, on voit que plusieurs sont influencés par un style oriental.

**L** En comparaison avec 1000, ce chevalier porte une jupe de mailles plus courte et des manches rallongées pour former des moufles avec une paume en tissu pour protéger les mains. Les mailles font le tour des jambes avec un entrelas sous le genou pour éviter que cette partie de l'armure pende. Un manteau est porté par dessus les mailles et on l'attache avec une ceinture à la taille. Le casque est cylindrique avec le dessus plat et une visière percée pour la ventilation. Les éperons en pointe sont courbés pour s'adapter á l'os de la cheville. Le bouclier est plus petit avec un dessus plot portant les armes de Robert FitzWalter.

## Farbtafeln

**A** Ein früher Ritter mit einem Zierhelm (bestehend aus einem Eisenrahmen, ausgefüllt mit Risenplatten und an der Spitze von einer Kappe zusammengehalten) und einem gespaltenem Panzerhemd. Das Schwert ist zierverschweißt und in einem zeitgenössischen Knauf. Dire Scheide aus lederbespanntem Holz ist in einem Winkel angegurtet, so daß der Ritter nicht darüber stolpern kann. Die zylindrischen Stecksporen waren in Nordwesteuropa üblich.

**B** Der Panzer bestand aus verbundenen Esenringen, wobei jeder Ring an vier andere angeschlossen war. Der Schuppenpanzer wurde durch ein Vernieten der Schuppen durch eine Segeltuchunterlage hindurch hergestellt. Lamellenpanzer wurden durch reihenweise Verschnürung von Platten hergestellt, wobei auch die Reihen miteinander verschnürt waren.

**C** Die Panzer-Halsberge ist vorne und hinten für bessere Beweglichkeit gespalten; es gibt eine Helmkappe und ein Visier. Der Segmenthelm ist der häufigste auf dem Bayeux-Wandteppich. Der Schild ist drachenförmig, und das Schwert wird unter dem Panzer getragen, zugänglich durch einen Schlitz.

**D** Wenige Helme und keine Helmfutter sind erhalten , aber diese Rekonstruktion zeigt das lederne Futterband mit dem Helmrand vernietet, und das Futter an das Band angenäht. Im 12. Jahrhundert wurden Helme, die aus einem einzigen Metallstück geschmiedet wurden, immer weiter verbreitet, während sich der leicht nach vorn zeigende Helmschirm erst im späteren 12. Jahrhundert entwickelte. Das 13. Jahrhundert sah dann den vollen Gesichtsschutz zum Nackenschutz hinzukommen – der Vorläufer des geschlossenen Helms, der in den 30er Jahren des 13. Jahrhunderts entwickelt wurde.

**E** Die Rekonstruktion dieses Drachenschildes ist rein hypothetisch, da keine Muster erhalten sind. Aus Holzplanken hergestellt, könnte er mit bemaltem Leder bespannt und mit Kantenumrahmung versehen gewesen sein. Der aus Eisen, Bronze oder Messing bestehende Helmbuckel war im Überbleibsel des Rundschildes und diente nur der Verzierung. Schilde des 12. Jahrhunderts hatten oft eine abgeflachte Oberseite und waren nach außen hin konvex.

**F** Ziergeschweißte Schwerter wurden aus Bündeln verdrehter, zusammengeschmiedeter Eisen- und Flaßstahlstäbe hergestellt, die gehämmert und weiter verdrecht wurden, bis die Schwertklinge entstand. Der Griff wurde geformt, indem man das Stichblatt bis zur Klingenschulter schob und darüber zwei Holzstücke miteinander verleimte. Der Knauf wurde darauf gesteckt. Lanzen wurden wahrscheinlich aus Eschenholz hergestellt, mit einer Eisenspitze und einem Anschlußstück für den Schaft. Die Flaggen stammen vom Bayeux-Wandteppich.

**G** Sättel waren sehr simpel. Ein aus zwei Stücken bestehender Sattelbaum befand sich zu beiden Seiten des Pferderückens, und die Sattelbogen waren so geformt, um sich einem Mittelausschnitt am unteren Rand anzupassen. Die Steigbügel waren lang, mit den Lederriemen unter den Sattelklappen geführt. Eine Satteldecke wurde verwendet, um Wundreiben zu verhindern. Die Sättel des 12. Jahrhunderts waren ähnlich, aber mit mehr aufrechter Hinterpausche; die Zäume hatten häufig kein Nasenband. Das Packpferd trug einen Sattel mit Packtaschen.

**H** Werkstätten waren wahrscheinlich aus Stein, um feuersicher zu sein. Handbetätigte Blasbälge fachten das Feuer an. Eine Fackel bot eine kontrollierbare Lichtquelle, bei deren Schein der Waffenschmied den Zustand des erhitzen Metalls an der Farbe erkennen konnte. Man sieht zwei Baumstümpfe – einer mit einem darin versenkten Amboß, der andere mit Löchern zur Aufnahme von Eisenstäben zum Aushämmern von Helmen.

**I** Ein Eber wurde Windhunden gestellt und wird nun von einem schwereren 'Alaunts' angegriffen. Der Ritter unterscheidet sich von den Knappen durch sein längeres Haar. Der Wildschweinspieß hat Zapfen, um sein zu tiefes Eindringen zu vermeiden.

**J** Im Jahre 1078 marschierte William I. gegen Gerberoi, um dort seinen Rebellensohn Robert zu belagern. Bei einem Ausfall Roberts aber wurde Williams Pferd getötet und der König verwundet. Der Engländer Toki hielt William und gab ihm sein eigenes Pferd; Toki wurde dann von einem Armbrutsc hützen tödlich getroffen. Für den König aber war der verlorene Kamp und obendrei der Sturz aus dem Sattel die größte Demütigung seines Lebens.

**K** Die Normannen hatten in Italien viel Erfolg gegen die Byzantiner, als sie diese mit einer soliden Reihe von Reitern mit eingelegten Lanzen angriffen. Viele Ritter trugen Rüstungen nach westlicher Art, viele andere aber waren beeinflußt von östlichen Formen.

**L** Im Vergleich zum Jahre 1000 trägt dieser Ritter einen verkürzten Panzerrock mit Ärmeln, die in Panzerfäustlinge mit Stoff-Handflächen verlaufen. Panzerstrümpfe mit einem Netz über dem Knie, um Rutschen zu verhindern. Ein Wappenrock wird mit Gürtel über der Rüstung getragen. Der Helm ist zylindrisch, mit flacher Oberseite und einem starren Gesichtsschutz, der für Belüftung durchbohrt ist. Die spitzige Sporen sind gekurvt, um das Sprungbein zu berücksichtigen. Der Schild ist kleiner, mit flacher Oberseite und mit dem Wappen von Robert FitzWalter.